Exploring Academic Ethics

Exploring Academic Ethics

STEVEN M. CAHN

RESOURCE *Publications* · Eugene, Oregon

EXPLORING ACADEMIC ETHICS

Resource Publications
An Imprint of Wipf and Stock Publishers
199 W. 8th Ave., Suite 3
Eugene, OR 97401

www.wipfandstock.com

PAPERBACK ISBN: 979-8-3852-3048-8
HARDCOVER ISBN: 979-8-3852-3049-5
EBOOK ISBN: 979-8-3852-3050-1

11/19/24

To my wife,
Marilyn Ross, MD

Contents

PART IV | A TEACHER'S RESPONSIBILITIES

Acknowledgments

THROUGHOUT THIS WORK I have adapted material from some of my previous books:

Cahn, Steven M., *The Eclipse of Excellence: A Critique of American Higher Education*. Public Affairs Press, 1973. Reprinted by Wipf and Stock Publishers, 2004.

———, *Education and the Democratic Ideal*. Nelson-Hall Company, 1979. Reprinted by Wipf and Stock Publishers, 2004.

———, *Saints and Scamps: Ethics in Academia*. Rowman and Littlefield, 1986; Revised Edition, 1994. 25th Anniversary Edition, 2011.

———, *Puzzles & Perplexities: Collected Essays*. Rowman & Littlefield, 2002. Second Edition, 2007.

———, *From Student to Scholar: A Candid Guide to Becoming a Professor*. Columbia University Press, 2008. Second Edition, Wipf and Stock Publishers, 2024.

———, *Teaching Philosophy: A Guide*. Routledge, 2018.

———, *The Road Traveled and Other Essays*. Wipf and Stock Publishers, 2019.

———, *Inside Academia: Professors, Politics, and Policies*. Rutgers University Press, 2019.

———, *Navigating Academic Life: How the System Works*. Routledge, 2021.

———, *Professors as Teachers*. Wipf and Stock Publishers, 2022.

I am grateful to Wipf and Stock Publishers for their support over many years. For this project, I especially wish to thank Savanah N. Landerholm for her expert typesetting and design.

My brother, Victor L. Cahn, playwright, critic, and professor emeritus of English at Skidmore College, edited many of these essays when they first appeared, and his innumerable suggestions are incorporated throughout. I am also indebted to Dr. Mary Ann McHugh, instructor in the Hugh Downs School of Human Communication at Arizona State University, for her skilled polishing of the manuscript. To my wife, I owe more than I can express.

One final note. This book's cover features an image of the Miller Library at Colby College in Waterville, Maine. Six decades ago, what was then called the Colby College Summer School of Languages offered study of French, German, Russian, and Spanish, each at the introductory, intermediate, and advanced levels. At meals, only the foreign language was spoken, and in the evening, cultural programs such as foreign language films and lectures on classical music were offered.

I may have established a record by attending three times to study three different languages: Russian to meet a college language requirement, then French and German for my doctorate. Outstanding instructors from various schools participated, and I was especially influenced by four inspired teachers: Igor Zelljadt (Russian—Smith College), George Pistorius (French—Williams College), Boris Nelson (German—University of Toledo), and Philip Bither (German—Colby College). Even though I originally came to Colby without a special interest or talent in foreign languages, these professors and the school's carefully structured program led me to an appreciation for the subject that has remained with me throughout my life.

While this book identifies moral shortcomings too often found in the practices of colleges and their faculties, the cover serves as a reminder that at its best higher education is an admirable enterprise that contributes to personal growth and, as we shall see, the success of democracy.

Introduction

In 1963, I embarked on a doctoral program in philosophy at Columbia University. At that time, the study of ethics focused on the meaning and justification of moral judgments and the strengths and weaknesses of various moral theories. I never heard the term "moral problems" and would not have had any idea to what it might have referred.

Before the end of that decade, however, the field changed dramatically. American philosophers, spurred by debate over the morality of the Vietnam War, broadened their understanding of the role of philosophy in public affairs. Once the War was deemed an appropriate subject for moral inquiry, so were other pressing matters, such as abortion, euthanasia, and world hunger.

Soon attention widened to include the ethical dimension of various professions. The activities of physicians, nurses, lawyers, business executives, journalists, and engineers were all subjected to scrutiny, and serious questions were raised about the degree of moral sensitivity displayed in hospitals, courts, and boardrooms. Professional schools began to take such concerns seriously and even added ethical theorists to their faculties. Indeed, today the staff of a hospital is likely to include not only MDs practicing their specialties but also PhDs concerned with questions of medical ethics.

Oddly, however, the moral issues inherent in one professional area have attracted little attention. Few philosophers have shown much interest in examining the moral problems arising in their own bailiwick: higher education. Some scholars apparently believe that the practices at colleges and universities and the actions of professors raise no ethical concerns—a dubious supposition. Other potential inquirers may be dissuaded from pursuing the subject by the discomfortable possibility of finding fault with their own institutions, their colleagues, or even themselves.

Furthermore, whereas hospital administrators and staff have welcomed the attention of moral philosophers, no such warm greeting would be expected from the typical college administrators or faculty. They would likely resist requests for reviews of their procedures or decisions and would defend their penchant for acting behind closed doors by appealing to the importance of confidentiality and academic freedom.

Thus, beginning in the 1970s while the literature in medical ethics flourished and studies in other fields of professional ethics grew, hardly any scholarship developed in the field I dubbed academic ethics. Then in 1986, Rowman & Littlefield published my book *Saints and Scamps: Ethics in Academia*. Revised in 1986 and reissued in an expanded 25th anniversary edition, this pioneering volume enumerates, explains, and emphasizes the most fundamental professorial obligations.

Subsequently, I invited colleagues across the country to write essays for a collection published in 1990 by Temple University Press titled *Morality, Responsibility, and the University: Studies in Academic Ethics*. I was gratified that fourteen well-known professors of philosophy, among them Robert Audi, Theodore M. Banditt, N. Ann Davis, Paul D. Eisenberg, Alan Gewirth, Alan H. Goldman, David Lewis, and Andrew Oldenquist, contributed articles on a wide range of topics, including academic freedom and tenure, sexual harassment, affirmative action, *in loco parentis* policies, and business-university partnerships.

In 1992, when Lawrence C. Becker edited the *Encyclopedia of Ethics* (Garland Publishing), I appreciated the opportunity to contribute an entry on academic ethics but realized that only a few years before the topic would not have been recognized as appropriate.

Nevertheless, the field needed further development; hence, I arranged with Rowman & Littlefield to publish a fifteen-volume series titled *Issues in Academic Ethics,* each volume combining an original monograph with supplementary sources, such as philosophical articles, legal opinions, or university documents that amplify the text. I list the books here by title, author, and date:

Campus Rules and Moral Community: In Place of In Loco Parentis
David A. Hoekema (1994)

Ethics of Scientific Research
Kristin Shrader-Frechette (1994)

Neutrality and the Academic Ethic
Robert L. Simon (1994)

A Professor's Duties: Ethical Issues in College Teaching
Peter J. Markie (1994)

University-Business Partnerships: An Assessment
Norman E. Bowie (1994)

Academic Freedom and Tenure: Ethical Issues
Richard T. De George (1997)

Diversity and Community in the Academy: Affirmative Action in Faculty Appointments
Celia Wolf-Devine (1997)

The Moral Dimension of Academic Administration
Rudolph H. Weingartner (1999)

Free Speech on Campus
Martin P. Golding (2000)

Sexual Harassment as a Ethical Issue in Academic Life
Leslie Pickering Francis (2001)

Moral Leadership: Ethics and the College Presidency
Paul J. Olscamp (2003)

Unionization in the Academy: Visions and Reality
Judith Wagner DeCew (2003)

Ethics and College Sports
  Peter A. French (2004)

Peer Review: A Critical Inquiry
  David Shatz (2004)

The Kindness of Strangers: Philanthropy and Higher Education
  Deni Elliott (2006)

While these books offer an inviting avenue to the study of academic ethics, I realized that what would be helpful would be a compact anthology suitable for classroom use. Therefore, in 2011 I edited *Moral Problems in Higher Education,* published by Temple University Press and reprinted in 2021 by Wipf and Stock Publishers. It offers essays on a variety of topics, including tenure, free speech on campus, sexual harassment, preferential student admissions, preferential faculty appointments, institutional neutrality, restrictions on research, peer review, letters of recommendation, and intercollegiate athletics. Among those whose work is included are William G. Bowen and Derek Bok, Myles Brand, Philip Kitcher, Charles R. Lawrence III, George Sher, Robert B. Talisse and Scott F. Aikin, Stephan Thernstrom and Abigail Thernstrom, Laurence Thomas, Nancy Tuana, and Robert Paul Wolff.

Then in 2022, sensing a need to provide more contemporary materials for discussion, I arranged with Rowman & Littlefield to publish an extensive collection of new essays in the field. Titled *Academic Ethics Today: Problems, Policies, and Prospects for University Life,* the volume contains thirty-one original articles, including an extensive foreword by Rebecca Newberger Goldstein and essays by Elizabeth Harman on racism and academic freedom, Mary Kate McGowan on free speech, Keota Fields on impediments to academic success, Christa Davis Acampora on artificial intelligence, Cynthia Stark on sexual harassment, Jennifer M. Morton on inequality, Ann E. Cudd on past injustice, James F. Keenan, SJ, on community colleges, Alexandra Bradner on the adjunct system, Karen Hanson on academic administration, Anita L. Allen on administrative discretion, Shelley Wilcox on remote teaching, Laura M. Howard on online instruction, Meira Levinson on college admissions, Bryan

Warnick on graduate school admissions, Anthony Simon Laden on the social costs of a college education, Dan Edelstein and Debra Satz on liberal education, Kyla Ebels-Duggan on an ethics requirement, and Harry Brighouse on undergraduate teaching.

I cite this array of names and issues to demonstrate the breadth of the field of academic ethics and the large number of distinguished scholars who have contributed to it. All their work centers on at least one of the two major aspects of the subject: professorial responsibilities and institutional policies. My book *Saints and Scamps* centers on the former; the recent collection *Academic Ethics Today focuses on the* latter.

While throughout my career I have written about many traditional philosophical topics, including free will, religious belief, and happiness, for over fifty years I have been concerned with academic ethics, and here I have collected my work on four matters that I have found of special interest: curricular controversies, tenure processes, affirmative action, and a teacher's responsibilities.

My hope is that this volume will bring increased attention to the field of academic ethics and highlight some of its most provocative issues.

PART I

Curriculum

I

Curricular Structure

WHILE STUDENTS AT MEDICAL school are required to learn anatomy, and students at law school are required to learn contracts, what should students pursuing a liberal arts degree be required to learn? The question may appear simple, but it leads to a clash between departmental and institutional concerns.

No one doubts that within departmental majors, requirements are appropriate. I have yet to hear anyone argue that mathematics majors should not have to learn calculus or that music majors should not have to learn harmony. After all, no student is forced to specialize in any field, but once that choice is made, the essentials of the subject need to be mastered. That much is uncontroversial.

But if a student chooses to pursue a liberal arts degree, one that is supposed to provide a basic, systematic understanding of our world, should any subject or skills be required?

Administrators are inclined to answer affirmatively. They seek a curriculum that is educationally justifiable and easily explainable. Although a few schools, such as Brown University, have made their selling point the freedom of students to create their own course of study, most educational leaders are uncomfortable admitting that they award BA degrees to those who have never encountered substantial materials from one or more of the major

3

fields of inquiry, including mathematics and the natural sciences, the social sciences, and the humanities.

Faculty members, however, recognize that instituting any requirement forces students to take courses in which they may have little or no interest, and teaching reluctant students is especially demanding. Working with students who have enrolled of their own accord is more inviting.

The difficulty with this convenient line of argument is that students may not select their courses wisely, thereby constructing a program that is either one-sided or muddled. Many faculty members are aware of this situation but believe that if students select courses foolishly, the problem is theirs. They are adults who have to live with the consequences of their choices.

The crux of the issue, however, is that the faculty, not the students, award diplomas stating that their holders have satisfactorily completed an appropriate course of study and consequently have been awarded a degree. Who declares that individuals have earned this honor? Do they sign their own diplomas? If so, the documents would be worthless. Instead, they are granted on the authority of the faculty and for that reason are recognized outside the college. Thus, the faculty's moral obligation is to ensure that students awarded degrees have acquired the relevant knowledge and skills that justify the recognition received.

To view the matter from a different perspective, consider a physician asked to sign a document attesting to your good health. Suppose you say to the doctor, "Don't bother with my heart. I know it's fine." Any physician worthy of the name will reply that if you want the doctor's signature, then the doctor decides how the examination should be conducted.

In the face of this reasoning, faculty members are tempted to avoid responsibility for establishing requirements by instituting an advisory system. Brown University, for example, states that "all students are matched with faculty and peer advisors who provide counsel on important academic decisions."[1]

---

1. "The College," Brown University, https://www.brown.edu/academics/college/.

Leaving aside the oddity of paying tuition to receive advice from another student (even one given the high-flown title of "peer advisor"), consider the following familiar scenario. A student wishes to register only for courses in the humanities. An advisor urges the student to take some work in the social and physical sciences, but the student balks. What to do? Different advisory systems offer different solutions.

Suppose students are permitted to disregard the recommendations of their advisor. Then the faculty will be committed to the irresponsible action of awarding degrees to students who have not acquired the essentials of a liberal education.

Imagine, however, that students are forced to adhere to rules imposed by a so-called advisor. Would students be subject to the same ruling if they were to switch advisors? If different advisors are empowered to impose different rules, then the system is unfair because one student might be forced to study a laboratory science while another might be permitted to substitute a course in science fiction. If, however, the rules are uniform across the school so that changing advisors is pointless, the result is, in effect, to abandon the advisory system and replace it with requirements.

Many faculty members are reluctant to think about curricular structure, preferring to concentrate on their own research. Awarding liberal arts degrees, however, to those who lack essential elements of a liberal education is akin to an inspector's certifying that an airplane with structural flaws is nevertheless in working condition. In both cases, not acknowledging problems is a moral failing.

2

Liberal Education

SOME ARGUE THAT LIBERAL education is the study of subjects of intrinsic rather than instrumental value, learned for their own sake, not a means to further ends. To cite one proponent of this view, liberal education is "beyond utility." Those who embrace this position are likely to speak longingly of the trivium and quadrivium (the subjects in a medieval education) while expressing far less concern about recent developments in physical and social science. In their eyes the curriculum is a museum for the wisdom of the past, preserved so as to avoid contamination from the laboratory or the marketplace. In the words of Eva T. H. Brann, the instructor at St. John's College whom I just quoted, "Our time is not an era in which the scene of learning can teem with much newness . . . .I believe that possibility began to vanish three centuries ago."[1] Thus, Brann believes that just about the time Newton was born, human creativity was exhausted.

Even those who do not share such antiquarianism may believe that the content of a liberal education is self-justifying. The fundamental flaw in this approach, however, was exposed long ago by John Dewey. Consider this comparatively neglected passage from his *Democracy and Education*:

1. Eva T. H. Brann, *Paradoxes of Education in a Republic* (Chicago: University of Chicago Press, 1979), 3, 62.

6

"We cannot establish a hierarchy of values among studies. In so far as any study . . . marks a characteristic enrichment of life, its worth is intrinsic . . . . Those responsible for planning and teaching the course of study should have grounds for thinking that the studies and topics included furnish both direct increments to the enriching of lives of the pupils and also materials which they can put to use in other concerns of direct interest."[2]

In other words, to argue that the content of liberal education is of intrinsic value and hence self-justifying provides no defense against the counterclaim that some alternative curriculum is also of intrinsic value and, therefore, also self-justifying.

Another common defense of liberal education appeals to such notions as self-fulfillment, self-cultivation, or self-realization. The suggestion is that these personal goals are most effectively achieved by study of the liberal arts.

This approach, though, faces serious problems. No matter how such terms are understood, Magnus Carlson achieved them by playing chess and Diana Taurasi by playing basketball. Yet neither of these activities is central to anyone's concept of a liberal education. On the other hand, a significant number who complete such an education are discontented, disaffected, or even disoriented.

A more promising defense emphasizes the usefulness of acquiring a basic understanding of our world. After all, studying the sciences, social sciences, and humanities helps us make sense of the human condition.

A difficulty with this line of argument, however, is that it fails to demonstrate why a liberal education is significant for the many who may lack the fervor to embark on a four-year quest for knowledge. Can the enormous amount of time and money that our society commits to education be justified as a glorious effort to enable millions to sip from the font of wisdom? In that case, prudence

2. John Dewey, *Democracy and Education: The Middle Works of John Dewey*, 1899–1924, ed. Jo Ann Boydston (Carbondale, Southern Illinois University Press, 1980), 9:248, 250.

might dictate that in light of our society's limited resources, we ought to provide a liberal education only to potential intellectuals while preparing all others for earning a living. Even if that policy is rejected as inconsistent with our country's commitment to equality of opportunity, the crucial issue is why a specialist needs a general education. For example, why should a future economist be required to study music, a future musician chemistry, or a future chemist economics?

Some proponents of liberal education respond by observing that the most useful preparation for any career is not job training. They argue that the concept of vocational education should be broadened to include scientific, historical, and ethical questions that illuminate any occupational path.

This reply is partially effective but does not demonstrate why an individual ought to study all the essentials of a liberal education. Granted, a future musician might be well advised to study French, German, or Italian, the philosophy of art, and even that branch of physics dealing with acoustics. But why chemistry or biology? Indeed, why any subject whose connection to music is remote?

The four previous justifications mistakenly rest the case for a uniform curriculum on factors differing from person to person. I suggest, instead, that we concentrate on our commonalities—in particular, our common responsibilities as free persons in a free society. After all, each of us is not only, for example, a farmer, an electrician, or a nurse but also a citizen, and the welfare of a democracy depends in great part on the understanding and capability of its citizenry. The reason for as many persons as possible to receive a liberal education is that it provides the knowledge, skills, and values all of us need to make a success of our experiment in self-government.

What are the essential knowledge, skills, and values?

In addition to possessing an understanding of the democratic system itself, every member of a democracy should be able to read and write effectively so as to be able to participate fully in the free exchange of ideas vital to an open society. Every member of a democracy should also be able to comprehend the range of public issues, from poverty, climate change, and ideological conflict to the dangers of nuclear warfare and the benefits of space research. These topics cannot be intelligently discussed by those ignorant of the physical structure of the world, the forces that shape society, or the ideas and events that form the background of present crises. Thus, every member of a democracy should possess substantial knowledge of physical science, social science, world history, and national history.

The study of science assumes familiarity with the fundamental concepts and techniques of mathematics, because such notions play a critical role in the physical sciences and an ever-increasing role in the social sciences. Furthermore, to know only the results of scientific and historical investigations is not sufficient; one needs also to understand the methods of inquiry that have produced these results. No amount of knowledge brings intellectual sophistication unless one also possesses the power of critical thinking. Every member of a democracy, therefore, should be familiar with the canons of logic and scientific method.

Still another characteristic that should be common to all members of a democracy is sensitivity to aesthetic experience. An appreciation of literature, art, and music enriches the imagination, refines the sensibilities, and increases awareness of our world. In a society of aesthetic illiterates, not only the quality of art suffers but also the quality of life.

In connection with literature, note that significant value is derived from reading a foreign literature in its original language. Not only does great literature lose some of its richness in translation, but learning another language increases linguistic sensitivity and makes one more conscious of the unique potentialities and limitations of any particular tongue. Such study is also a most effective means of widening cultural horizons. Understanding another language is a key to understanding another culture.

Every member of a democracy should also acquire intellectual perspective, the ability to scrutinize the fundamental principles of thought and action, encompassing both what is and what

9

ought to be. The path to such wisdom lies in the study of those subtle analyses and grand visions that comprise philosophy. No other subject affords a stronger defense against intimidation by dogmatism while simultaneously providing a framework for the operation of intelligence.

Thus, we arrive at a justification for the study of liberal education. The more who undertake it, the better, for the ignorance of some is a threat to all. If anyone complains that our democracy provides too much education for too many, they reveal their misunderstanding of a democratic society, for how can the electorate be too educated, too knowledgeable, or too astute? As a result of inadequate education, however, democracy may disappear.

3

Academic Politics

WHILE I WAS CHAIRING the philosophy department at the University of Vermont, the college undertook a search for a new dean of arts and sciences. When the finalists came to campus, department heads were invited to interview them, and I decided to ask every candidate the same two questions. My first: "Should our graduates have a basic understanding of the physical structure of the world?" Each candidate agreed confidently that they should. Then I continued: "Can I therefore assume that you favor a science requirement for the bachelor's degree?" Almost all candidates suddenly faltered, seeking some way to reconcile their support for the study of science with their worries about requiring it. Only one candidate, chemist John G. Jewett, responded directly: "I do favor a science requirement, plus a mathematics requirement."

Later at an informal reception, one of my colleagues approached Jewett and expressed concern about his answer.

"I'm unsure about your idea to increase requirements. Don't you think we should proceed cautiously?"

"Why?" said Jewett. "Do you have another plan?"

"No," said my colleague.

"Then why not try mine?"

I was pleased when Jewett was appointed to the position, and decades later the college still has a requirement that undergraduates study both mathematics and science. (Incidentally, I once heard the late longtime chair of the philosophy department, William E. Mann, describe Jewett as the "scourge of those who despise merit.")

Instituting requirements, however, is invariably a struggle. Regardless of how strongly the administration may favor them, the faculty decide the matter and bear the burden of implementing any plan. Hence, the needed consensus is always elusive.

Indeed, any faculty meeting that considers requirements is inevitably raucous, and the pattern of debate is all too predictable. First, the head of the school's curriculum committee introduces a motion to the effect that all students be required to study a laboratory science, a foreign language, or perhaps the history of Western civilization. Regardless of the specific content of the motion, one sincere soul soon takes the floor to deliver a rambling speech that concludes resignedly with the rhetorical question, "But why should we place such restrictions on our students?"

The meeting then turns into chaos as the original motion is buried under an avalanche of amendments to the motion, substitute motions, and amendments to the substitute motions. Hours later, when exhaustion sets in, a survivor of the marathon session moves to table the entire matter. Amid sighs of relief, this motion passes (thankfully it is undebatable), the meeting is adjourned, faculty members stagger out of the auditorium, and on each succeeding graduation day, students receive their diplomas without having had to demonstrate any knowledge of a laboratory science, a foreign language, or the history of Western civilization.

Several factors contribute to deadlock. To begin with, professors are specialists, and for most, the central concern is their own field, not anyone else's. This point was emphasized for me at a meeting of the head of graduate programs at the City University of New York when a dean was discussing the difficulties faced by the biology program and inquired whether anyone had ideas for solving the problem. The head of English raised his hand and said, "I don't know what to suggest, but I have to say candidly that I don't care about biology. If it collapses, so be it. My only concern is English."

Given that such an attitude is widespread among faculty members, why would they want to institute requirements that would force their students to study subjects about which the faculty themselves are unconcerned? In fact, some of the faculty may have studied those subjects in school and done poorly.

A college friend of mine who excelled in all his courses once said to me, "People are as proud of their intellectual weaknesses as of their strengths." Think for example, how often you have heard someone say with pride, "I can't do math" or "I'm not a scientist." A faculty member may have a profound knowledge of the Victorian novel yet long ago have given up trying to learn mathematics or science. Why, then, would such a professor favor a requirement in those areas?? Analogously, some faculty members have virtually no knowledge of classical music. Why would they support a rule that all students, in order to receive a college degree, need to study Bach, Beethoven, Brahms, and Bartok?

One other factor may be the most important. How much support departments receive from the administration depends on student enrollments. As class sizes rise, the department's case for a new appointment is strengthened; if the numbers decline, the department may not be permitted to fill a vacancy. Hence, an issue on everyone's mind is how any proposed requirement would affect each department's enrollment. For example, if a foreign language requirement is instituted, more students have to enroll in foreign-language courses, thus affecting other departments negatively. Only if a change in requirements is seen as neutral or favorable to a department would its members be willing to consider the proposal.

As a result, trading requirements is a common practice. If I support a science requirement, will you support a history requirement? Therefore, the details of a successful curricular plan are likely to include anomalies that result not from fundamental principles but from departmental self-interest. Thus does academic politics undermine the faculty's moral responsibility to ensure that those awarded a liberal arts degree have completed the essentials of a liberal education.

4

Distribution Requirements

THE MOST OBVIOUS WAY to gain faculty support for ensuring that students bring some semblance of balance to their choice of classes is to divide the curriculum into areas, then require a certain number of courses in each. Because this system favors no department and requires no faculty members to devote their time to developing new offerings, this plan is the easiest to pass. Referred to as a distribution requirement, it is the most common curricular structure in American colleges.

Consider, for example, Williams College, an eminent liberal arts school where the so-called divisional requirement classifies courses into three areas: language and the arts, social studies, and science and mathematics.[1] Language and the arts includes art history, art studio, classics, comparative literature, dance, English, foreign languages, music, and theatre. Social studies includes anthropology, cognitive science, economics, history, philosophy, political science, psychology, religion, and sociology. Science and mathematics includes astronomy, biology, chemistry, computer science, maritime studies, mathematics, neuroscience, physics, and statistics. Students must complete at least three courses from each area, thereby obtaining some breadth.

1. "Areas of Study," Williams College, http://www.williams.edu/academics -p/areas-of-study/.

The difficulties with this approach, however, are obvious. Because students have innumerable courses in each division from which to choose, the result may still be a remarkably narrow education. For instance, a student could fulfill the language and the arts requirement by taking drawing, photography, and costume design, then graduating with a liberal arts degree without having studied literature or a foreign language. Similarly, a student could fulfill the social studies requirement by taking the New Testament, earliest Christianities, and the development of Christianity, then graduating without having studied economics, political science, sociology, or religions other than Christianity. Analogously, a student could fulfill the science and mathematics requirement by taking only courses in statistics and none in science.

In addition, the areas themselves are somewhat arbitrary. After all, is a course in philosophy of art not related to the study of art? And is symbolic logic not allied with mathematics? Yet both philosophy of art and symbolic logic are classified under philosophy, which is filed under social studies. Furthermore, why can students graduate without a course in history or philosophy but not without a course in language or the arts? Perhaps academic politics was originally involved, but few may remember.

In any case, the advantages of such a curriculum redound to faculty members, who can assure themselves that each student has taken courses across the curriculum, while professors teach the same courses they would have offered even if no requirements were in place. In addition, no department stands to gain or lose enrollment from the requirement. As a result, the administration can announce a structured curriculum, students can take virtually whatever they want, and the faculty can focus on their specializations.

In this way, the faculty may irresponsibly award a student a liberal arts degree who has no knowledge beyond the high school level in literature, history, science, foreign language, and music or art, as well as no notion of issues in economics, political science, sociology, or philosophy. To quote the British philosopher J. L.

Austin, writing in another context: "These seem to be rather serious deficiencies."[2]

To avoid them, why not increase the number of areas, then restrict the courses in each that fulfill the requirement? Thus, treat language and the arts as two areas not one, and require courses in both literature and arts. Then restrict the acceptable courses to those that offer appropriate depth and breadth. For example, an Introduction to English literature would count; Hollywood films would not. The latter is an appropriate subject for study, but given that students may take only one course in the area of literature, I doubt that most English professors would urge students to study movies rather than Shakespeare, George Eliot, or James Joyce.

The most extreme version of a distribution requirement would be for the areas to be numerous and the courses to be limited, even to the extent of one course per area. In such a case the pressures on the faculty to offer the required courses would be strong, and only a group conscious of its moral obligations would undertake such a program. Nowadays such an approach is rarely, if ever, found, but I am familiar in detail with at least one historical precedent.

When I came to New York University (NYU) in 1968, I found the record of a recent curriculum that today would strike faculty and students as astounding. A major figure in the implementation of this remarkable course of study was philosopher Sidney Hook, who was joined by a cadre of extraordinary scholar-teachers, including mathematician Morris Kline, physicist Morris Shamos, political scientist Rita Cooley, and many others who were determined to fulfill the faculty's responsibility by presenting required subjects so as to display their importance to all students. Nor only were requirements instituted, but they were defended in extensive essays found in the school's catalogue.

Here, in their own words, is a brief description of the curriculum they developed in the 1950s for what was called the Unified Studies Division of Washington Square College of Liberal Arts

2. J. L. Austin, *Sense and Sensibilia* (Oxford: Oxford University Press, 1963), 54.

and Sciences. All students spent their first two years fulfilling these requirements, then pursued a conventional major.

Competent writing and reading are essential to all other studies and for most occupations in later life; therefore, a basic course in English fundamentals is given in the freshman year. This course is followed by one in the literature of Western Europe, introducing the students to their literary heritage. European culture is explored further in a one-term course in the history and literature of Greece and Rome.

A full-year history course then surveys the major developments—political, social, economic, and cultural—that mark the changing fortunes of European civilization from the decline of Rome to the present. A one-term course in philosophical analysis acquaints the students with the great philosophical systems in Western culture and introduces them to the techniques of philosophical thinking.

Because of the interest in the arts and because of their place in the development of civilization, students take a year-long course in the history of either music or art.

International communication in all fields of knowledge, as well as in political and business relations, has become increasingly important and urgent. In consequence, the College requires that before graduation every student should have a reasonable command of one foreign language.

Four one-term courses in the social sciences introduce the student to sociology, the picture of the social structure in which we live; psychology, the study of human experience and behavior; government, the theory, operation, and politics of the America political system compared with other systems; and economics, the study of how people make a living.

Science and mathematics are essential parts of a modern liberal arts education; the basic values inherent in both go far beyond the practical significance attained by them in modern times. The science segment of the program is designed to give the student these values without, however, inserting the detail needed by the specialist. The sequence begins with a one-term course in mathematics, followed by a term of physical science. The student then pursues a one-term laboratory course in either biology, chemistry, geology, or physics.[3]

In the late 1960s, this curriculum, like so many others of the time, was destroyed, then replaced by a weak distribution requirement. Although not many schools ever offered such an exemplary program as that developed at NYU, today's faculty members would be surprised if they went to their school library and found a catalogue from the 1950s. Invariably, the curriculum described there demands far more of both students and faculty than the school's current curriculum.

In fact, in the early 1970s, while at NYU teaching a large course in philosophy of education, I experimented by announcing in class that some faculty members had urged instituting a new curriculum. Without revealing the source, I described the NYU plan from five years before. My students were aghast and complained that no one could handle so much material. Then I revealed that although this curriculum was not likely to be instituted, it was the exact one completed by their older brothers and sisters who had graduated recently from NYU. Much had been asked from them, and they met those expectations. Lowering aspirations, however, is likely to produce less accomplishment.

3. New York University, *New York University Bulletin: Washington Square College of Arts and Sciences,* 1965–1966 (New York: New York University, 1965), 30. Minor change have been made for the sake of uniformity.

5

A Core Curriculum

DISTRIBUTION REQUIREMENTS, WHETHER LAX or demanding, rely for the most part on courses chosen from departmental offerings. By their very nature, however, these reflect single disciplines.

Suppose a faculty develops a multidisciplinary plan that calls on instructors from various fields to pool their efforts and provide all beginning students, before their choice of major, with the same foundation for a liberal education. That plan is known as a core curriculum, and nowadays it is a rarity.

A longest-standing, exemplary one is offered at my alma mater, Columbia College, the relatively small, co-educational liberal arts college within Columbia University. Even though the essentials of the College's program date back to the first half of the twentieth century, they are not widely known. Yet the model is so remarkable that I want to outline it, hoping that doing so may be helpful in thinking about curricular options.[1]

While undergraduates at Columbia may choose from more than eighty majors, over forty concentrations, and hundreds of electives, all students are required to take not only a one-semester course in expository writing, four semesters of a foreign language, two semesters of science, and two semesters from the global core

1. "Academic Requirements," Columbia College, http://www.bulletin.columbia.edu/columbia-college/requirements-degree-bachelor-arts/.

(comparative studies), but also the following five courses of the Core Curriculum:

- Introduction to Contemporary Civilization in the West (two semesters)
- Masterpieces of Western Literature and Philosophy (two semesters)
- Masterpieces of Western Art (one semester)
- Masterpieces of Western Music (one semester)
- Frontiers of Science (one semester)

The oldest part of the Core is Contemporary Civilization, developed in 1919 to inquire into issues of war and peace. In the school's words, the course aims "to introduce students to a range of issues concerning the kind of communities—political, social, moral, and religious—that human beings construct for themselves and the values that inform and define such communities; the course is intended to prepare students to become active and informed citizens."[2]

While the reading list changes over time, here is a recent one:

FIRST SEMESTER

- Plato, *Republic* (entire)
- Aristotle, *Nicomachean Ethics and Politics*
- Hebrew Bible, *Exodus* 1–24; *Deuteronomy* 1–6; *I Samuel* 8–10, 17–20; *Ecclesiastes* (entire)
- New Testament, *Matthew* 3–7; *Romans* (entire); *Galatians* (entire)
- Augustine, *City of God*
- *Quar'an*

2. "About Contemporary Civilization," Columbia College, http://www.college.columbia.edu/core/classes/cc.php.

- Medieval Philosophy (selections by Ibn Tufayl, Al-Ghazali, and Thomas Aquinas)
- Machiavelli, *The Prince*
- New World (selections by Sepulveda and Vitoria)
- Protestant Reformation (selections edited by Hans Hillerbrand)
- Scientific Revolution (selections by Descartes)
- Hobbes, *Leviathan*
- Locke, *Second Treatise*

SECOND SEMESTER

- Rousseau, *Discourse on Inequality and Social Contract*
- Smith, *Treatise on Moral Sentiments*
- Kant, *Groundwork of the Metaphysics of Morals*
- Smith, *Wealth of Nations*
- Burke, *Reflections on the Revolution in France*
- Wollstonecraft, *A Vindication of the Rights of Woman*
- Tocqueville, *Democracy in America*
- Mill, *On Liberty*
- Mill and Taylor, *The Subjection of Women*
- Elizabeth Cady Stanton, "Address to the Legislature of New York"
- Sojourner Truth, "Ain't I a Woman?"
- Marx, selection from the *Marx-Engels Reader*
- Darwin, *Origin of Species* and *Descent of Man*
- Nietzsche, *On the Genealogy of Morals*
- Du Bois, *The Souls of Black Folk* and "Souls of White Folk"
- Freud, selections from the *Freud Reader*
- Gandhi, "Swaraj"(On self-rule)

- Fanon, "On Violence" in *The Wretched of the Earth*
- Foucault, *Discipline and Punish*

This course is taught in sections of twenty to twenty-five students and requires faculty members from different departments to cooperate in the planning and staffing. The result differs from any single department's offerings.

The same is true of Literature Humanities, which dates back to 1937. In the school's words, it "is designed to enhance students' understanding of main lines of literary and philosophical development that have shaped western thought for nearly three millennia. Much more than a survey of great books, Lit Hum encourages students to become critical readers of the literary past we have inherited. Although most of our Lit Hum works (and the cultures they represent) are remote from us, we nonetheless learn something about ourselves in struggling to appreciate and understand them."[3] Again, the course is taught in small sections with instructors from a range of departments.

Here is a recent reading list. All works are read in their entirety, except as noted:

FIRST SEMESTER

- Homer, *Iliad*

- Sappho, *Lyrics*

- Homer, *Odyssey*

- Hebrew Bible, *Genesis*

- Herodotus, *The Histories* (selections)

- Aeschylus, *Orestia*

- Euripides, *Bacchae*

- Thucydides, *History of the Peloponnesian War* (selections)

---

3. "About Literature Humanities," Columbia College, http://www.college.columbia.edu/core/lithum/about.

- Plato, *Symposium*
- Vergil, *Aeneid*
- Ovid, *Heroides* (selection)

SECOND SEMESTER

- New Testament, in *Luke* and *John*
- Augustine, *Confessions*
- Dante, *Inferno*
- Boccaccio, *Decameron* (selections)
- Montaigne, *Essays*: "To the Reader"; "On Idleness"; "On the Power of the Imagination"; "On Cannibals"; "On Repentance"; "On Experience"
- Shakespeare, *King Lear*
- Cervantes, *Don Quixote* (selections)
- Milton, *Paradise Lost*
- Austen, *Pride and Prejudice*
- Dostoevsky, *Crime and Punishment*
- Woolf, *To the Lighthouse*
- Morrison, *Song of Solomon*

Faculty members who teach this course go beyond their field of specialization, and students, regardless of their future majors, build a foundation for further reading.

A skeptic might wonder what an undergraduate student learns from reading a work such as the *Inferno*. The best answer I ever heard was given years ago at a public event where the core curriculum was being celebrated. An instructor told the story of a student's coming into her office to complain, "I'm not getting anything out of Dante." To which she replied, "The issue is not what you're getting out of Dante; the issue is what Dante is getting out of you." Or, as the College writes, "Lit Hum encourages us to compare our own assumptions and values to the radically different ones expressed in our readings. It demands that we examine ourselves in relation to our past." In short, if reading Dante did not encourage self-reflection, the fault lay not with Dante but with the student. (I still recall that in Dante's monumental vision, the greatest sin was treachery to benefactors, and the greatest sinners, held in the three mouths of Lucifer at the bottom of hell, were Brutus, Cassius, and Judas Iscariot.)

Moving to another curricular area, I would emphasize that Columbia Core is rare, perhaps unique, in requiring the study of both art and music. If students are given a choice, they almost invariably pick the area they know best, whereas they would surely learn more by enrolling in the other. Columbia, however, doesn't offer the option.

Art Humanities became part of the Core in 1947, and in the school's own description "is not a historical survey, but an analytical study of a limited number of monuments and artists, and teaches students how to look at, think about, and engage in critical discussion of the visual arts."[4] A typical semester explores in detail the Parthenon, Amiens Cathedral, and the work of Raphael, Michelangelo, Pieter Bruegel, Gian Lorenzo Bernini, Rembrandt van Rijn, Francisco Goya y Lucientes, Claude Monet, Pablo Picasso, Frank Lloyd Wright, Le Corbusier, Jackson Pollock, and Andy Warhol. The course also makes extensive use of New York City through field trips to museums, buildings, and monuments.

Music Humanities, also introduced in 1947, according to the College "has awakened in students an appreciation of music in the Western world, it has helped them respond intelligently to a variety of musical idioms, and it has engaged them in the debates about the character and purposes of music that have occupied composers and musical thinkers since ancient times."[5]

The general outline is as follows:

4. "Art Humanities," Columbia College, http://www. arthum.college.colum bia.edu/.

5. Music Humanities, Columbia College, http://www. college.columbia. edu/core/classes/mh.php.

MEDIEVAL AND RENAISSANCE MUSIC

- Gregorian chant
- Hildegard of Bingen
- Josquin des Prez
- the madrigal

BAROQUE MUSIC

- Monteverdi
- Handel: *Messiah*
- Bach: the Brandenburg Concertos

CLASSICAL MUSIC

- Haydn instrumental works
- Mozart operas and instrumental works
- Beethoven symphonies

ROMANTIC MUSIC

- Schubert (the Lied)
- Chopin
- Berlioz: *Symphonie fantastique*
- Wagner
- Verdi

TWENTIETH-CENTURY MUSIC

- Debussy
- Stravinsky: *The Rite of Spring*

- Berg: *Wozzeck*
- Schonberg

AMERICAN COMPOSERS

- Ives
- Copland
- Cage

JAZZ

- Armstrong
- Ellington
- Parker

Like Art Humanities, Music Humanities is taught in small sections and takes advantage of cultural life in New York City. Attending a concert or opera may be routine for some students, but for many others the course takes them to places they never would have gone and offers them experiences they never would have enjoyed. Not surprisingly, as a result of having taken this course, many Columbia students develop a lifetime devotion to music.

One advantage of requiring the art and music courses is that students do not face the intimidating prospect of learning either subject surrounded by those already passionate about it. Here most are beginners, and the course is structured with them in mind.

Frontiers of Science was added to the core in 2004. As the course is described, "it is designed to instill skills more generally characteristic of the scientific approach to inquiry, in the context of several scientific disciplines." A recent semester's subjects included "elements of neuroscience, astrophysics, Earth science, and biodiversity . . . .The first two put larger questions of reality, our place in the Universe, and who we are as humans into scientific context. The Earth science and biodiversity modules connect to important societal issues."[6] Frontiers of Science combines a one-day-a-week lecture by a researcher with weekly seminars "to discuss the lecture and associated readings, to undertake in-class activities, and to debate the implications of the most recent scientific discoveries."[7] Like the other Core courses, Frontiers of Science calls on faculty from different departments to teach across disciplinary boundaries.

Note that the primary beneficiaries of a core curriculum are the students, not the faculty. No wonder, then, that the strongest supporters of the Columbia core are the alumni, who recognize the value of having been provided with a breadth of vision that illuminates any subsequent specialization.

Granted, other schools make a virtue of encouraging students to follow their own interests, wherever they may lead. But these often develop haphazardly, without systematic exploration of available alternatives. What students happen to find interesting may be the result of suggestions from relatives or friends, the influences of the media, or the effects of good or bad teaching in elementary and secondary schools. Perhaps a family subscription to *Psychology Today* sparked an interest in that subject, while a roommate's bad experience in a philosophy course discouraged the pursuit of that inquiry. To consider a more pointed example, a monomaniacal premed student may be interested only in the natural sciences, believing work in the social sciences or humanities irrelevant to a physician's responsibilities.

Such cases illustrate that for a first-year student to be asked to choose sensibly from thousands of available classes is an unfortunate situation that arises from the faculty's failure to meet its responsibilities by constructing and teaching courses that provide the fundamentals of a liberal education. How much easier for faculty members to leave matters to the students, even if they are unprepared to make a wise choice. They may waste time and money while the professors continue their research undisturbed.

6. "Welcome," Frontiers of Science, Columbia College, http://www.ccnmtl. columbia.edu/projects/frontiers/.

7. "Frontiers of Science," Columbia College, http://www. college. columbia. edu/core/classes/fos.php.

To see the problem vividly, just show Columbia's Literary Humanities reading list to a a professor of literature and ask if studying the works listed is worth a student's time. Almost all faculty members will answer affirmatively. Then ask: Would you be willing to teach a course with this reading list? Almost all will refuse, preferring to teach only their own fields of specialization. Therein lies the problem of creating a strong curricular structure.

In conclusion, you may wonder why for decades many of Columbia's faculty have been willing to contribute their time and effort to ensure that students who are awarded liberal arts degrees have received a liberal arts education. Analogously, we might ask why some members of society give of themselves to provide support to those who need it. The answer lies in altruism, a disinterested concern for the welfare of others. Show me a college with a carefully structured curriculum, and I'll show you a faculty that takes its moral responsibilities seriously.

PART II

Tenure

6

The Tenure System

FACULTY MEMBERS WHO POSSESS tenure hold lifetime appointments, revocable only in rare instances of gross incompetence or moral turpitude. Yet reference to this prerogative invariably gives rise to the same questions: Why should anyone receive permanent job security? Doesn't tenure pamper the indolent and protect the incompetent?

Academic tenure is not as singular as often supposed. In most organizations of university size, employees, whether at lower ranks or in middle management, are rarely dismissed for cause. Due to poor performance, they may be passed over for promotion, given lateral transfers, or occasionally demoted, but they are rarely discharged. While plant closings or fiscal crises may precipitate worker layoffs, tenured professors, too, face the loss of their positions if a department is phased out or a school closes.

Even the mechanics of the tenure system are hardly unique. Consider large law firms that routinely recruit new associates with the understanding that after several years they will either be offered some variety of permanent position or required to depart. Colleges make similar arrangements with their beginners.

Despite such analogies, however, tenure undoubtedly provides professors an unusual degree of latitude and security. They are privileged to explore any area of interest and proceed in whatever manner they wish. No one may dictate to them that certain subjects are taboo, that certain methods of inquiry are illegitimate, or that certain conclusions are unacceptable.

Tenure thus guarantees academic freedom, the right of all qualified persons to discover, teach, and publish the truth as they see it within their fields of competence. Where academic freedom is secure, students enter classrooms with the assurance that instructors are espousing their own beliefs, not mouthing some orthodoxy they have been programmed to repeat.

Although widely seen as valuable, academic freedom is threatened whenever anyone seeks to stifle free inquiry in the name of some cause that supposedly demands everyone's unthinking allegiance. Some, for example, have sought to have a school adopt an official stance on issues unrelated to its educational mission. Free inquiry, however, is impeded when certain opinions are officially declared false and others true. Colleges and universities are not established to inform the public where a majority of the faculty stands on any issue, be it mathematical, scientific, or political. Whether an argument for the existence of God is sound or our government's foreign policy misguided are matters for discussion, not decree.

Maintaining free inquiry requires that all points of view be entitled to a hearing. Unfortunately, some both from inside and outside academia have occasionally attempted to interfere with a campus speaker's presentation on the grounds that they find unpalatable the views expressed. So long as the lecturer remains respectful of others, however, no one at the school, be they professors, students, or administrators, should block any individual from expressing ideas. No matter how noxious they may be, the greater danger lies in stifling them, for when one person's opinion is silenced, no one else's may be uttered in safety.

But might academic freedom be preserved without tenure, perhaps by some form of multi-year contracts? The problem besetting any alternative scheme is that it could too easily be misused, opening faculty members to attack because of their opinions.

A key feature of the tenure system is that those who hold tenure decide whether it should be granted to others. Thus, those who judge are not facing a conflict of interest because their own tenure is not at stake. In any system of multi-year contracts, however, the question arises: Who should decide whether a contract ought to be renewed? If the decision is placed in the hands of other tenured professors, they would be voting while realizing that their own contracts would eventually be up for renewal. The result would be a conflict of interest. After all, if I support your renewal, will you support or oppose mine? Worse, the decision might be made by administrators with an ax to grind, favoring contract renewal for professors who have aided administrative initiatives. Such a system would produce an atmosphere of suspicion and recrimination, antithetical to independent thinking.

Unquestionably, the tenure system has dangers, but none as great as those that would attend its abandonment. To adapt a remark about democracy offered by Winston Churchill, tenure may be the worst form of academic governance except all those other forms that have been tried from time to time.

To defend the tenure system in principle, however, is not to applaud all the ways it has been implemented. Sometimes, instead of individuals being required to demonstrate why they deserve tenure, a department has been expected to demonstrate why they don't. In court a person ought to be presumed not guilty until the evidence shows otherwise, but in matters of special skill you ought not be supposed qualified until so proven. A school's failure to observe this guideline results in a faculty encumbered with deadwood, and more than a few departments suffer from this unfortunate phenomenon.

Yet tenure decisions can present difficult problems and have been known to cause hostilities that last for decades. Unpleasant as events may become, though, faculty members need to act conscientiously because the future of their departments and schools are at stake. Even a single ill-advised decision may lead to years of disruption and possible decay, bringing tenure itself into disrepute and thereby threatening that academic freedom the system is intended to preserve.

7

Criteria for Tenure

WHAT ARE THE APPROPRIATE criteria for tenure decisions? Traditionally, three aspects of a faculty member's record are considered: scholarship, service, and teaching.

As to scholarship, it is widely recognized as an arduous undertaking. It requires not only engaging in research but publishing the results in scholarly articles and books. Even reading papers at professional conferences, while commendable, is insufficient because a scholar's original thinking needs to be available for scrutiny by experts, and the easiest way for them to have access is for material to be published. Scholarly writing need not be elegant (it rarely is), but it is expected to be precise. Scholars cannot merely approximate the views they are trying to express; what they say needs to be formulated exactly.

Work counts most heavily if it is subject to peer review. University presses typically require that manuscripts be approved by at least two outside experts, and professional journals depend on evaluations by at least a couple of scholars, typically using "blind review," in which the referee does not know the identity of the author. The local newspaper may request a professor's thoughts on events of the day, but no other scholars have examined the ideas to determine if they merit publication. A professor may even publish a best-selling book, but assuming that it has not been peer reviewed, it will be given far less weight than if it had been published by a relatively minor university press that relies on the judgments of experts.

As for the criterion of service, it typically involves participation in departmental committees, such as those overseeing the curriculum, student awards, library holdings, and so on. Other activities might be serving on a school-wide committees dealing with curricular and degree requirements, helping the admissions office by evaluating applications, lecturing to a campus group, or representing the institution at a national conference. In any case, each member of a faculty is expected to assume a fair share of the day-to-day tasks that are an inescapable part of academic life.

Service, however, is not afforded the importance given to research, a disparity apparent in the methods by which each is evaluated. In the case of research, an elaborate review is undertaken, including faculty reading the candidate's research as well as sending it out for judgments by experts in the field. In the case of service, the activities are merely listed on an individual's record; quantity is noted, whereas quality is rarely of concern.

Teaching is the third criterion in a tenure decision. It should be judged with the same care as research but too often is treated more like service.

If teaching were taken more seriously, evaluating it would involve input from departmental colleagues who would visit the professor's classes and assess syllabi, examinations, and test papers to analyze teaching performance. Indeed, an outsider or two, experienced in observing teachers, might be asked to attend a couple of classes and write reviews.

Instead, courses an individual has taught are merely listed and supplemented by packets of student evaluations. The issue is not whether the professor excelled in the classroom but whether the performance was so subpar that it causes concern. This lack of emphasis on the importance of teaching in making tenure decisions is a key reason why the quality of college teaching is too often disappointing, failing to provide students with the quality of instruction that they were promised and to which they are entitled.

Yet relying heavily on student evaluations of teaming is un-justified. Some of its proponents have argued that students are the best evaluators of their own responses, drawing an analogy to the restaurant patron who is a better judge of the food than the chef. But while those who eat know how the food tastes, a nutritionist most reliably judges its nutritional benefit, just as educators most reliably know educational value.

Students who by definition have not mastered the subject are poorly situated to know how well it is being taught. Perhaps they find a concept challenging. Is the instructor to blame or is the material inherently difficult?

Granted, students are a convenient source for easily verifiable matters such as whether teachers hold class regularly, speak at an understandable pace, encourage class participation, maintain interest, return examinations without delay, provide detailed comments on term papers, appear at announced office hours, and so on. Students, however, are not in a position to recognize whether faculty are knowledgeable or their presentations reliable.

Furthermore, evaluating an instructor primarily on the basis of student opinion is not only inappropriate but also dangerous. As Charles Frankel observed, "Teaching is a professional relationship, not a popularity contest. To invite students to participate in the selection or promotion of their teachers . . . exposes the teacher to intimidation."[1] No professor should be put in a position in which advantage is gained by granting students a favor in exchange for their support.

Corporate executives judge other corporate executives to decide promotions in a company, and attorneys judge other attorneys to decide partnerships in a law firm. Likewise, professors should judge other professors to decide matters such as reappointment, promotion, and tenure. Indeed, no professionals should shirk the responsibility of judging their colleagues. To do so is not only inappropriate but inimical to the interests of those supposedly served. After all, if a quack is practicing surgery in a hospital, who is to

1. Charles Frankel, *Education and the Barricades* (New York: Norton, 1968), 30–31.

blame, the patients or other physicians? If an incompetent is lecturing at a university, the ones at fault are not the students but the other professors. They are responsible for systematically observing classes and gaining insight into what is occurring.

Faculty rightfully claim authority in the academic sphere. When the time comes for evaluating teaching, they should not abandon their duty.

8

Tenure Decisions

TO SEE HOW TENURE decisions should be made, consider two hypothetical cases, then three factual ones. Taken together, they clarify the importance of appropriate balancing of criteria.

Imagine that Adam comes to Eastern College to begin a professorial career. During his first two years, he gains experience teaching standard departmental offerings while struggling with and finally finishing his dissertation, which he and his advisor had optimistically estimated he would complete before his arrival. In his third and fourth years he devotes himself to planning several new courses and participating in an exciting multidisciplinary program. While reasonably successful as a teacher, he publishes two articles derived from his dissertation. In his fifth and sixth years, he continues to enjoy rapport with students while publishing a couple of book reviews and another article, this one based on a seminar paper written in graduate school. He has also begun work on what he hopes will be a book-length manuscript, but the project is still at an early stage.

In his sixth year, in accordance with the principles of the American Association of University Professors, a decision needs to be made on Adam's tenure. He is liked by his students, has various publications, and is at work on a major scholarly project. He is a cooperative colleague and has participated enthusiastically in multidisciplinary activities. Should he be awarded tenure?

Doing so involves excessive risk, for Adam's most productive years may lie behind him. He has not demonstrated the capacity for sustained, creative effort, and a careful examination of his bibliography raises serious doubts whether he has produced any significant scholarship since his dissertation. His good rapport with students may be based more on a beginner's enthusiasm and spirit of camaraderie, possibly short-lived, rather than on fundamental pedagogic skills and enduring qualities of mind that would sustain his teaching in later years. Peer review, if used, may even have raised some doubts in this direction. His contributions to the life of the school may decline when the novelty of such activity wanes, and in time he may no longer be familiar with the frontiers of his own field. If he is awarded tenure, then fulfills our worst fears, those who suffer most will be the generations of students forced to endure his premature academic senility.

Admittedly, were he retained he might in the long run prove a significant asset to the college. That outcome, though, is only a possibility, not a probability. For the sake of future students as well as in the interest of each academic discipline, every effort should be made to appoint and retain only those individuals who, compared to all other available candidates, are most likely to achieve excellence. Adhering to such a rigorous standard is the surest way to avoid the succession of egregious and irremediable errors that are the likely consequences of laxity.

Adam's supporters, however, can be depended on to argue that the evaluations of his record have placed too much emphasis on the criterion of publication. After all, they may remind us, one great teacher wrote nothing: Socrates. Those who appeal to his case tend to overlook that the Athenian gadfly spent his life in public debate, befuddling the cleverest minds of his time, forcing them to rethink their fundamental commitments. Few would doubt the scholarly qualifications of any professor who could do the same. But as Socrates himself pointed out, impressing students and friends is no guarantee of one's acumen.

Adam's supporters will claim that despite his thin publication record, he has proven himself a good teacher. But is he merely competent, or is he so outstanding that we have strong reason to suppose that replacing him in the classroom would significantly reduce the quality of instruction? Unless the latter were the case, an individual should be appointed in his stead who would at least match him as a teacher while surpassing him as a scholar. After all, why should a college award tenure to a present member of the faculty if other persons more capable stand ready to serve?

In the face of this challenge, Adam's supporters are apt to retreat to the view that, while his credentials are admittedly borderline, we ought nevertheless give him the benefit of the doubt, taking into account the extra hours he has spent with students, the favors he has done for colleagues, and, above all, the disturbance and distress a rejection would cause him. Those responsible for tenure decisions should never succumb to such pleadings; they are obliged to remember Sidney Hook's observation that "most . . . tenured faculty who have lapsed into apparent professional incompetence . . . were marginal cases when their original tenure status was being considered, and reasons other than their proficiency as scholars and teachers were given disproportionate weight."[1] The principle should be "when in doubt, say no," a policy that will not be popular with Adam, his family, or his friends. But only by maintaining rigorous standards for the awarding of tenure can an institution safeguard its academic quality.

Adam's record might be summarized as follows: good but not excellent teaching, good but not excellent service, and fair scholarship. This record does not justify the granting of tenure.

Next consider Eve, who begins her teaching career at Western University. Her dissertation, completed prior to her arrival, is published by a leading university press. Throughout the next five years, she contributes substantial articles to major professional journals, and months before she is to be considered for tenure, another well-regarded academic publisher accepts her second book.

1. Sidney Hook, *Education and the Taming of Power* (La Salle, IL: Open Court, 1973), 213.

Yet her teaching record is far less successful. Students complain that her lectures are bewildering and that she is rarely available for consultation outside class. Registration for her courses is small, although a few advanced students have signed up repeatedly. Peer review, if in use, may have revealed that she speaks in a monotone while peering out the window. Her presentations reflect a firm grasp of the most recent literature but are convoluted and fail to motivate most students. She has reluctantly agreed to serve on several departmental committees but has little to say at the meetings. Should she be awarded tenure?

Her teaching is not good, and her service unimpressive. How strong is her scholarship? If the evidence indicates that no one is available who matches the quality of her research, then she has a case to receive tenure. Her teaching, however, presents a serious problem. Perhaps she could work only with advanced students and not be placed in introductory courses. If, however, she cannot be trusted to be effective at any level, then awarding her tenure is irresponsible because even a university that puts the highest premium on research is morally obligated to provide students with competent instruction.

Her situation might be summarized as follows: research outstanding, teaching weak, and service unimpressive. Only if outside experts agree that she is a scholar with unquestionable national or international impact might she deserve to be granted tenure.

Here's a third case, and this one has a factual basis. Linda (a pseudonym) was a fine teacher with a thin record of publications. Her service, though, was extraordinary. She chaired innumerable department and school-wide committees, displaying tact and insight. She spent countless hours preparing reports, planning conferences, and developing curricula. In many ways she was the heart and soul of her department and a crucial member of the college faculty. She was universally admired. Should she have received tenure?

Her situation might be summarized as follows: research thin, teaching strong, and service extraordinary. A replacement could have been found who would have been more heavily published and perhaps equally adept in the classroom, but no applicant could have been expected to display her skill and commitment in dealing with people as well as her dedication and success in contributing to the welfare of her department and school.

In fact, she was denied tenure. I believe that decision was a mistake, and eventually her colleagues realized their error. By then, however, she had changed careers and climbed high on the corporate ladder.

Here's another actual case. The following account was authored by the late Paul J. Olscamp, a philosopher who served as president of Western Washington University (1975–1982), then of Bowling Green University (1982–1995). So far as I know, the narrative is factual, but I am not aware of who was involved or where the events occurred.

> Dr. Sally Morse (a fictitious name) found herself standing for tenure and promotion to associate professor. Her department was targeted by her university as a "niche" discipline—a discipline or set of disciplines in a single department that the university wished to develop into a major player in the state's research environment. Expectations and rewards were higher for this department than for all others in the university. Morse submitted her application in her sixth year as a faculty member. Her teaching evaluations were excellent. She had few refereed publications, although the ones she had were in journals of high repute. Morse's service record was barely adequate, but the department informed the collegiate-level tenure and promotion committee that this was because the department discouraged her service activities and encouraged research in its place.
>
> Morse's research and publication record was clearly good enough to have earned her tenure in almost all the university departments not designated as "niche." But it was average in comparison to the records of similar applicants from other "niche" programs. In a split vote within her department (6–4 with one abstention), she was recommended for tenure and promotion. Included

in her file was a letter from the chair noting that Morse's research protocol was proceeding on schedule, and that the majority of the published work from her project could not be expected until her work was complete. It was also noted that Morse had not attracted significant outside funding from either government or private sources.

On the basis of the department split vote, the collegiate-level tenure and promotion committee voted 5–4 to deny her tenure and promotion. The committee noted that this decision was particularly difficult for them because in most other departments her record would have qualified her for tenure and promotion. They also noted the systematic vagueness in the university's standards of excellence with respect to the three evaluative criteria (teaching, research, and service).

The dean of the college recommended that Morse be given tenure but that promotion to associate professor be withheld pending further publication of her research. In his recommendation, the dean noted the split vote of the collegiate committee and their comments on the vagueness of the evaluative criteria. He stated that if "niche" programs were to have higher standards, then the departmental policies should say that and define them.

The university-level tenure and promotion committee overturned the dean's recommendation, agreeing with the collegiate committee, but once again by a split vote, and with the same reservations expressed by the dean.

Olscamp now turns from factual description to an attempted justification of the ultimate decision.

> It was clear that the expectations of Morse were much higher than the average for tenure and promotion applicants for the university as a whole. It was also clear that the higher criteria she had to meet were nowhere clearly defined in university policy. Given her record to date, it was reasonably foreseeable that Morse would continue to develop in her research as well as in other professional categories.
>
> Morse was a superstar teacher, and even in a niche department the school could not afford to lose such a

fine instructor without violating its promises to students and their parents.

Olscamp concludes by sharing the outcome:

> Dr. Sally Morse was given tenure and promoted. The policies and procedures manuals are being revised to correct the deficiencies noted by the committees. The work is still in progress, having proven much more difficult than was anticipated.[2]

The most noticeable feature of this case was Morse's weak support from her colleagues. In the absence of personal animosity, most departmental members are reluctant to deny tenure to colleagues with whom they have worked closely for years. In this case, however, only six out of eleven supported Morse. The college-level tenure and promotion committee voted against tenure, as is uncommon, and the Dean clearly had doubts, recommending tenure but not promotion, an unusual procedure because the two usually go together. The university-level tenure and promotion committee also voted against tenure, thereby overturning the dean's recommendation, a rare occurrence. As for Morse's research, although she was informed at the outset that it should be her first priority, she had few publications and did not attract outside funding, an important criterion for success in most science and some social science departments. That her record was good enough compared to members of other departments is irrelevant because those faculty were not provided with the support she had received.

Regarding her teaching, she received excellent student evaluations, but why did those qualify her as a "superstar" teacher? Apparently, no peer evaluations were used. Furthermore, how many teachers received equally strong evaluations? Would someone else teaching her classes significantly reduce quality of instruction? If not, she could be replaced by someone who would at least have matched her as a teacher while surpassing her in scholarly output.

2. Paul J. Olscamp, *Moral Leadership: Ethics and the College Presidency* (Lanham, MD: Rowman & Littlefield, 2003), 43–47. The material has been edited for the sake of consistency.

Remember that for every opening, hundreds of applications are received, and retaining her was preventing numerous others from being considered.

In addition, her service was described as "barely adequate," but that failing was excused because she was supposed to focus on research. Yet service can take various forms, many of which are not especially time-consuming, and her not finding some way to help her colleagues was a mark against her.

Olscamp presents the case for awarding her tenure, but to my mind his arguments fall short. He claims that her research would develop and might in the long run yield publications, but who knows? If those being considered for tenure do not publish when the pressure to do so is greatest, why assume they will do so when the strongest incentive has been removed? He also stresses that criteria for tenure in niche departments were not given with specificity, but he does not say that the situation differed in other departments. In fact, whenever experts assess quality, no simple formula can replace human judgment. Whether an athlete merits admission to a hall of fame, a pianist deserves a prize at a music competition, or a movie is worthy of an award at a film festival is a decision that goes beyond mere numbers, and the same is the case for granting tenure. No wonder that, as Olscamp relates, the attempt to revise the policies and procedures manual proved much more difficult than anticipated. I doubt the work was ever completed.

The strangest feature of the case is that Morse was ultimately awarded tenure not because of any scholarly contribution but because of her supposed status as a "superstar" teacher. Her performance in the classroom may have fit that description, but Olscamp offers no evidence beyond excellent student evaluations. Were her colleagues impressed by observing her teaching or at least hearing her present lectures? How strong was registration in all her courses? If the case for her tenure depended on her supposedly offering superb instruction, why wasn't more done to assess it?

Extraordinary performance as a teacher can justify the awarding of tenure but the case has to be overwhelming. Morse's was not; here's one that was.

Beginning in the 1960s, Robert Gurland taught philosophy at NYU. He published little, and while at the request of administrators he spoke to many university and outside groups, he was not active on departmental or schoolwide committees. Yet while his colleagues would teach ten or twenty students in a course, he would, no matter the subject, always teach over two hundred. On the first day of registration, his classes filled, and the demand invariably far exceeded the number of available seats. Students, regardless of their gender, race, ethnicity, or level of sophistication, flocked to his classes. He reciprocated the students' passion by knowing the name of everyone in every class, learning something about each, and personally grading, with numerous detailed comments, every one of the hundreds of papers.

He welcomed colleagues to observe his classes even without giving him prior notice, and, in light of the skepticism of some about the source of his popularity, he invited anyone who wished to review the exams he gave, the answer booklets his students submitted, and the grades he awarded (which were not especially generous). All who watched him teach and scrutinized the written record came away impressed. He taught virtually every course in the curriculum, from epistemology to ethics, from symbolic logic to medieval philosophy, from existentialism to philosophy of sport. No area of the subject was outside his purview, and occasionally he created courses when a new area of the subject developed.

Admittedly, he had a most engaging personality, a wonderful sense of humor, and an unusual background that included stints as a baseball player on local club teams and a professional trumpeter in leading jazz bands, as well as having had extensive experience teaching mathematics and science in elementary school, junior high school, and high school.

On one occasion when I asked him to explain his remarkable success, he opened his battered briefcase and held up stacks of yellow pads filled with writing. He explained that these were his lectures, and although he never looked at them during his classes, he knew exactly what material he was going to cover and how it would be presented. Even his vivid examples were written down. In short, his seemingly freewheeling style was carefully planned.

He won teaching awards at a variety of levels and institutions, but such honors meant far less to him than the enthusiastic response of his students. They included many of the school's best undergraduates, a number of whom, influenced by him, became highly successful philosophy professors. For two years he taught full-time at West Point. There he was such a hit with the cadets that he was offered a permanent position but turned it down to remain at NYU.

His situation might be summarized as follows: publications weak, service limited, and teaching phenomenal. Had he been replaced, the department could no doubt have found a stronger researcher who would have offered more consistent service on committees, but the quality of his teaching could not have been matched or even approached. Had he been replaced, student registration in the department would have plummeted, because he taught a massive percentage of all the students taking philosophy courses.

To no one's surprise, he received tenure. Generations of students were the beneficiaries of that wise decision.[3] As an outstanding researcher may be awarded tenure even with a weak performance in the classroom, so tenure should also be available to an outstanding teacher with a thin record of research. Granted, the ideal candidate excels as both researcher and teacher, but just as an occasional exception is made so as not to lose a researcher of national stature, an occasional exception should also be made so as not to lose a teacher of extraordinary accomplishment.

Few teachers can attain such a level of excellence; after all, taking the lead in developing a new multidisciplinary program, teaching a course that invariably has a high enrollment, offering extra help to struggling students, or attracting crowds to office

---

3. Regarding his impact, see *Bronx Socrates: Portrait of a Legendary Teacher*, ed. Steven M. Cahn (Eugene, OR: Wipf and Stock Publishers, 2024).

hours does not by itself overcome a thin record of research. Nevertheless, a faculty member with a superlative record of teaching, unlikely to be matched by any possible replacement, should be considered a strong candidate for a tenured appointment.

Note that a corollary of serious evaluation of teaching is the willingness to differentiate among levels of effectiveness. We recognize the difference between scholarship that is weak, mediocre, strong, or superb; the same distinctions apply to teaching. Not every accomplished researcher is a serious candidate for a Nobel Prize or its equivalent; neither is every sound teacher a serious candidate for the Teaching Hall of Fame. Describing all teachers as "good" or "not so good" is a sign that teaching is not taken seriously. An individual may be said to be a good teacher, but "how good?" is a key question.

In sum, if the case for tenure relies heavily on meeting only one of the three criteria, that category needs to be filled in spectacular fashion. If the case depends heavily on only two of the criteria, then they should both be filled with unquestionable excellence. If the case depends, as most do, on meeting each of the three criteria, then they should all be filled with high quality. Anything less or even borderline, and the department should begin a new appointment process.

Finally, let me mention an alternative approach to granting tenure that some find appealing. I refer to the proposal to create two sorts of professorships: one in research and one in teaching. Then the criteria for tenure in the two cases would be vastly different.

I do not favor this idea. The motto "publish or perish" may not appeal to some, but few who oppose it would object to the demand that faculty "think or perish"; yet to publish is to make available to all the results of one's best thinking. Professors who fail to do so should be expected to seek alternative ways of providing substantial evidence of their intellectual vigor. If they are unable to shoulder the burden of proof, others are justified in doubting the quality of their thinking and hence their teaching.

As for those who excel in scholarship, they should be encouraged to communicate their insights in a classroom. A professor, as the word's medieval Latin origin "professare" suggests, is one who makes open declarations. Taking the time to motivate, organize, and clarify one's thinking so as to share it with others never harmed anyone and can help students, who, after all, contribute to supporting the professor's way of life.

Instituting two classes of instructors would not enhance but diminish the importance of teaching, suggesting that it is not an activity worth the time and effort of prestigious professors. That message is surely the wrong one.

In sum, tenure decisions determine the quality of a department, faculty, and school. Giving each case the most careful consideration and always acting on principle is a faculty's obligation. After all, wise choices are a blessing, foolish ones a blight.

PART III

Affirmative Action

9

Two Concepts
of Affirmative Action

IN MARCH 1961, LESS than two months after assuming office, President John F. Kennedy issued Executive Order 10925, establishing the President's Committee on Equal Employment Opportunity. Its mission was to end discrimination in employment by the government and its contractors. The order required every federal contract to include this pledge: "The contractor will not discriminate against any employe[e] or applicant for employment because of race, creed, color, or national origin. The contractor will take affirmative action to ensure that applicants are employed, and that employe[e]s are treated during employment, without regard to their race, creed, color, or national origin."

Here, for the first time in the context of civil rights, the government called for affirmative action. The term meant taking appropriate steps to eradicate the then widespread practices of racial, religious, and ethnic discrimination.[1] The goal, as the President stated, was "equal opportunity in employment." In other words,

---

1. A comprehensive history of one well-documented case of such discrimination is Dan A. Oren, *Joining the Club: A History of Jews and Yale* (New Haven and London: Yale University Press, 1985). Prior to the end of World War II, no Jew had ever been appointed to the rank of full professor in Yale College.

procedural affirmative action, as I shall call it, was instituted to ensure that applicants for positions would be judged without any consideration of their race, religion, or national origin. These criteria were declared irrelevant. Taking them into account was forbidden.

The Civil Rights Act of 1964 restated and broadened the application of this principle. Title VI declared: "No person in the United States shall, on the ground of race, color, or national origin, be excluded from participation in, be denied the benefits of, or be subjected to discrimination under any program or activity receiving Federal financial assistance."

Before one year had passed, however, President Lyndon B. Johnson argued that fairness required more than a commitment to such procedural affirmative action. In his 1965 commencement address at Howard University, he said, "You do not take a person who for years has been hobbled by chains and liberate him, bring him up to the starting line of a race and then say, 'you're free to compete with all the others,' and still justly believe that you have been completely fair."

Several years later, President Johnson issued Executive Order 11246, stating, "It is the policy of the Government of the United States to provide equal opportunity in Federal employment for all qualified persons, to prohibit discrimination in employment because of race, creed, color or national origin, and to promote the full realization of equal employment opportunity through a positive, continuing program in each department and agency." Two years later the order was amended to prohibit discrimination on the basis of sex.

While the aim of President Johnson's order is stated in language similar to that of President Kennedy's, President Johnson abolished the Committee on Equal Employment Opportunity, transferred its responsibilities to the Secretary of Labor, and authorized the Secretary to "adopt such rules and regulations and issue such orders as he deems necessary and appropriate to achieve the purposes thereof."

Acting on this mandate, the Department of Labor in December 1971, during the administration of President Richard M.

Nixon, issued Revised Order No. 4, requiring all federal contractors to develop "an acceptable affirmative action program," including "an analysis of areas within which the contractor is deficient in the utilization of minority groups and women, and further, goals and timetables to which the contractor's good faith efforts must be directed to correct the deficiencies." Contractors were instructed to take the term "minority groups" to refer to "Negroes, American Indians, Orientals, and Spanish Surnamed Americans." (No guidance was given as to whether having only one parent, grandparent, or great-grandparent from a group would suffice to establish group membership.) The concept of "underutilization," according to the Revised Order, meant "having fewer minorities or women in a particular job classification than would be reasonably be expected by their availability." "Goals" were not to be "rigid quotas," but "targets reasonably attainable by means of applying every good faith effort to make all aspects of the entire affirmative action program work."

Such preferential affirmative action, as I shall call it, requires that attention be paid to the same criteria of race, sex, and ethnicity that procedural affirmative action deems irrelevant. Is such use of these criteria justifiable in employment decisions?

Return to President Johnson's claim that a person hobbled by discrimination cannot in fairness be expected to be competitive. How are we to determine which specific individuals are entitled to a compensatory advantage? To decide each case on its merits would be possible, but this approach would undermine the argument for instituting preferential affirmative action on a group basis. For if some members of a group are able to compete, why not others? Thus, defenders of preferential affirmative action maintain that the group, not the individual, is to be judged. If the group has suffered discrimination, then all its members are to be treated as hobbled runners.

Note, however, that while a hobbled runner, provided with a sufficient lead in a race, may cross the finish line first, giving that person an edge prevents the individual from being considered as fast a runner as others. An equally fast runner does not need

55

an advantage to be competitive. This entire racing analogy thus encourages stereotypical thinking. For example, recall those men who played in baseball's Negro Leagues. That these athletes were barred from competing in the Major Leagues is the greatest stain on the history of the sport. While they suffered discrimination, these players were as proficient as their counterparts in the Major Leagues. They needed only to be judged by the same criteria as all others, and ensuring such equality of consideration is the essence of procedural affirmative action.

Granted, if individuals are unprepared or ill-equipped to compete, then they ought to be helped to try to achieve their goals. Such aid, however, is appropriate for all who need it, not merely for members of particular racial, sexual, or ethnic groups.

Victims of discrimination deserve compensation. Former players in the Negro Leagues ought to receive special consideration in the arrangement of pension plans and any other benefits denied these athletes due to unfair treatment. The case for such compensation, however, does not imply that present Black players vying for jobs in the Major Leagues should be evaluated in any way other than their performance on the field. To assume their inability to compete is derogatory and erroneous.

Such considerations have led recent defenders of preferential affirmative action to rely less heavily on any argument that implies the attribution of non-competitiveness to an entire population.[2] Instead, the emphasis has been placed on recognizing the benefits society is said to derive from encouraging expression of the varied experiences, outlooks, and values of members of different groups.

This approach makes a virtue of what has come to be called "diversity."[3] As a defense of preferential affirmative action, diver-

2. See, for example, Leslie Pickering Francis, "In Defense of Affirmative Action," in *Affirmative Action and the University: A Philosophical Inquiry*, ed. Steven M. Cahn (Philadelphia: Temple University Press, 1993), 3–4. She raises concerns about unfairness to those individuals forced by circumstances not of their own making to bear all the costs of compensation, as well as injustices to those who have been equally victimized but are not members of specified groups.

3. The term gained currency when Justice Lewis Powell, in his pivotal

sity has at least two advantages. First, those previously excluded are now included not as a favor to them but as a means of enriching all. Second, no one is viewed as hobbled; each competes on a par, although with varied strengths.

Notice that diversity requires preferential hiring. Those who enhance diversity are to be preferred to those who do not. Those preferred, however, are not being chosen because of their deficiency; the larger group is deficient, lacking diversity.

What does it mean to say that a group lacks diversity? Or to put the question another way, could we decide, for example, which members of a ten-person group to eliminate in order to decrease most markedly its diversity?

So stated, the question is reminiscent of a provocative puzzle in *The Tyranny of Testing*, a 1962 book by the scientist Banesh Hoffman. In this attack on the importance placed on multiple-choice tests, he quotes the following letter to the editor of the *Times* of London:

> Sir—Among the "odd one out" type of questions which my son had to answer for a school entrance examination was: "Which is the odd one out among cricket, football, billiards, and hockey?" [In England "football" refers to the game Americans call "soccer," and "hockey" here refers to "field hockey."] . . . I said billiards because it is the only one played indoors. A colleague says football because it is the only one in which the ball is not struck by an implement. A neighbor says cricket because in all the other games the object is to put the ball into a net . . . . Could any of your readers put me out of my misery by stating what is the correct answer?

A day later the *Times* printed the following two letters:

> Sir.—"Billiards" is the obvious answer . . . because it is the only one of the games listed which is not a team game.

---

opinion in the Supreme Court's 1978 *Bakke* decision, found "the absence of a diverse student body" to be a goal that might justify the use of race in student admissions. An incisive analysis of that decision is Carl Cohen, *Naked Racial Preference* (Lanham, MD: Madison Books, 1995), 55–80.

Sir.—football is the odd one out because . . . it is played with an inflated ball as compared with the solid ball used in each of the other three.

Hoffman then continued his own discussion:

When I had read these three letters it seemed to me that good cases had been made for football and billiards, and that the case for cricket was particularly clever . . . At first I thought this made hockey easily the worst of the four choices and, in effect, ruled it out. But then I realized that the very fact that hockey was the only one that could be thus ruled out gave it so striking a quality of separateness as to make it an excellent answer after all—perhaps the best. Fortunately, for my piece of mind, it soon occurred to me that hockey is the only one of the four games that is played with a curved implement.

The following day the *Times* published yet another letter, this from a philosophically sophisticated thinker.

Sir.—[The author of the original letter] . . . has put his finger on what has long been a matter of great amusement to me. Of the four—cricket, football, billiards, hockey—each is unique in a multitude of respects. For example, billiards is the only one played with more than one ball at once, the only one played on a green cloth and not on a field . . . .

It seems to me that those who have been responsible for inventing this kind of brain teaser have been ignorant of the elementary philosophical fact that every thing is at once unique and a member of a wider class.

With this sound principle in mind, return to the problem of deciding which member of a ten-person group to eliminate in order to decrease most markedly its diversity. Unless the sort of diversity is specified, the question has no rational answer.

In searches for college and university faculty members, we know what sorts of diversity are typically of present concern: race, gender, and certain ethnicities. Why should these characteristics be given special regard?

Consider, for example, other nonacademic respects in which prospective faculty appointees can differ: age, religion, nationality, regional background, economic class, social stratum, military experience, bodily appearance, physical soundness, sexual orientation, marital status, ethical standards, political commitments, and cultural values. Why should we not seek diversity of these sorts?

To some extent schools do. Many colleges and universities indicate in advertisements for faculty positions that the schools seek veterans or person with disabilities. The City University of New York requires all searches to give preference to individuals of Italian-American descent.

The crucial point is that the appeal to diversity never favors any particular candidate. Each one adds to some sort of diversity but not another.

Suppose the suggestion is made that the sorts of diversity to be sought are those of groups that have suffered discrimination. This approach leads to another problem, clearly put by John Kekes:

> It is true that America Blacks, Native Americans, Hispanics, and women have suffered injustice as a group. But so have homosexuals, epileptics, the urban and the rural poor, the physically ugly, those whose careers were ruined by McCarthyism, prostitutes, the obese, and so forth . . .
>
> There have been some attempts to deny that there is an analogy between these two classes of victims. It has been said that the first were unjustly discriminated against due to racial or sexual prejudice and that this is not true of the second. This is indeed so. But why should we accept the suggestion . . . that the only form of injustice relevant to preferential treatment is that which is due to racial or sexual prejudice? Injustice occurs in many forms, and those who value justice will surely object to all of them.[4]

Kekes's reasoning is cogent. In addition, another difficulty looms for the proposal to seek diversity only of groups that have suffered discrimination. For diversity is supposed to be valued not

4. John Kekes, "The Injustice of Strong Affirmative Action," in Cahn, 151.

as compensation to the disadvantaged but as a means of enriching all. Consider a department in which most of the faculty members are women. In certain fields, for example, nursing, dental hygiene, and elementary education, such departments are common. If diversity by gender is of value, then such a department, when making its next appointment, should prefer a man. Yet men as a group have not been victims of discrimination. To achieve valued sorts of diversity, the question is not which groups have been discriminated against but which valued groups are not represented. The question thus reappears as to which sorts of diversity are to be most highly valued. I know of no compelling answer.

Seeking to justify preferential affirmative action in terms of its contribution to diversity raises another difficulty, for preferential affirmative action is commonly defended as a temporary rather than a permanent measure.[5] Preferential affirmative action to achieve diversity, however, is not temporary. Suppose it were. Then once an institution had appointed an appropriate number of members of a particular group, preferential affirmative action would no longer be in effect. Yet the institution may later find that it has too few members of that group. Because lack of valuable diversity is presumably no more acceptable at one time than another, preferential affirmative action would have to be reinstated. Thereby it would in effect become a permanent policy.

Why do so many of its defenders wish it to be only transitional? They believe the policy was instituted in response to irrelevant criteria for appointment having mistakenly been treated as relevant. To adopt any policy that continues to treat essentially irrelevant criteria as relevant is to share the guilt of those who discriminated originally. Irrelevant criteria should be recognized as such and abandoned as soon as feasible.

Some defenders of preferential affirmative action argue, however, that an individual's race, gender, or ethnicity is germane

---

5. Consider Michael Rosenfeld, *Affirmative Action and Justice: A Philosophical and Constitutional Inquiry* (New Haven and London: Yale University Press, 1991), 336: "Ironically, the sooner affirmative action is allowed to complete its mission, the sooner the need for it will altogether disappear."

to fulfilling the responsibilities of a faculty member. They believe, therefore, that preferential affirmative action should be a permanent feature of search processes because it takes account of criteria that should be considered in every appointment.

At least three reasons have been offered to justify the claim that those of a particular race, gender, or ethnicity are well-suited to be faculty members: first, they would be especially effective teachers of any student who shares their race, gender, or ethnicity;[6] second, they would be particularly insightful researchers because of their experiencing the world from distinctive standpoints;[7] third, they would be role models, demonstrating that those of a particular race, gender, or ethnicity can be effective faculty members.[8]

Consider in turn each of these claims. As to the presumed teaching effectiveness of the individuals in question, no empirical study supports the claim.[9] But even if compelling evidence were presented, it would have no implications for individual cases. A person who does not share race, gender, or ethnicity with students might teach them superbly. An individual of the student's' own race, gender, or ethnicity might be ineffective. Regardless of statistical correlations, what is crucial is that individuals be able to teach effectively all sorts of students, and seeking people who give evidence of satisfying this criterion is entirely consistent with procedural affirmative action. But knowing an individual's race, gender, or ethnicity does not reveal whether that person will be effective in the classroom.

6. See, for example, Francis, 31.

7. See, for example, Richard Wasserstrom, "The University and the Case for Preferential Treatment," *American Philosophical Quarterly*, 13(4),1976,165–170.

8. See, for example Joel J. Kupperman, "Affirmative Action: Relevant Knowledge and Relevant Ignorance," in Cahn, 181–188.

9. Consider Judith Jarvis Thomson, "Preferential Hiring," *Philosophy & Public Affairs*, 2(4), 1973, 368: "I do not think that as a student I learned any better, or any more, from the women who taught me than from the men, and I do not think that my own women students now learn any better or any more from me than they do from my male colleagues."

Do members of a particular race, gender, or ethnicity share a distinctive intellectual perspective that enhances their scholarship? Celia Wolf-Devine has aptly described this claim as a form of "stereotyping" that is "demeaning." As she puts it, "A Hispanic who is a Republican is no less a Hispanic, and a woman who is not a feminist is no less a woman."[10] Furthermore, are Hispanic men and women supposed to have the same point of view in virtue of their common ethnicity, or are they supposed to have different points of view in virtue of their different genders?

If our standpoints are thought to be determined by our race, gender, and ethnicity, why not also by the other numerous significant respects in which people can differ, such as age, religion, sexual orientation, and so on? Because each of us is unique, can anyone else share my point of view?

That my own experience is my own is a tautology that does not imply the keenness of my insight into my experience. The victim of a crime may as a result embrace an outlandish theory of racism. But neither who you are nor what you experience guarantees the truth of your theories.

To be an effective researcher calls for discernment, imagination, and perseverance. These attributes are not tied to one's race, gender, ethnicity, age, or religion. Black scholars, for example, may be more inclined to study Black literature than are non-Black scholars, but some non-Black literary critics are more interested in and more knowledgeable about Black literature than are some Black literary critics. Why make decisions based on fallible racial generalizations when judgments of individual merit are obtainable and more reliable?

Perhaps the answer lies in the claim that only those of a particular race, gender, or ethnicity can serve as role models, exemplifying to members of a particular group the possibility of their success. Again, no empirical study supports the claim, but it has often been taken as self-evident that, for instance, only a woman can be a role model for a woman, only a Black for a Black, and

10. Celia Wolf-Devine, "Proportional Representation of Women and Minorities," in Cahn, 230.

only a Catholic for a Catholic. In other words, the crucial feature of a person is supposed to be not what the person does but who the person is.

The logic of the situation, however, is not so clear. Consider, for example, a Black woman who is a Catholic. Presumably she serves as a role model for Blacks, women, and Catholics. Does she serve as a role model for Black men, or can only a Black man serve that purpose? Does she serve as a role model for all Catholics or only for those who are Black? Can I serve as a role model for anyone else because no one else shares all my characteristics? Perhaps I can serve as a role model for everyone else because everyone else belongs to at least one group to which I belong.

Putting aside these conundrums, the critical point is supposed to be that in a field in which discrimination has been rife, a successful individual who belongs to the discriminated group demonstrates that members of the group can succeed in that field. Obviously, success is possible without a role model, for the first successful individual had none. But suppose persuasive evidence were offered that a role model, while not necessary, sometimes is helpful not only to those who belong to the group in question but also to those prone to believe that no members of the group can perform effectively within the field. Role models would then both encourage members of a group that had suffered discrimination and discourage further discrimination against the group.

To serve these aims, however, the person chosen would need to be viewed as having been selected by the same criteria as all others. If not, members of the group that has suffered discrimination as well as those prone to discriminate would be confirmed in their common view that members of the group never would have been chosen unless membership in the group had been taken into account. Those who suffered discrimination would conclude that it still exists, while those prone to discriminate would conclude that members of the group lack the necessary attributes to compete equally.

How can we ensure that a person chosen for a position has been selected by the same criteria as all others? Preferential affirmative action fails to serve the purpose because by definition it differentiates among people on the basis of criteria other than performance. The approach that ensures merit selection is procedural affirmative action. It maximizes equal opportunity against every form of discrimination.

The policy of appointing others than the best qualified has not produced a harmonious society in which prejudice is transcended and all enjoy the benefits of self-esteem. Rather, the practice has bred doubts about the abilities of those chosen while generating resentment in those passed over.

Procedural affirmative action had barely begun before it was replaced by preferential affirmative action. The difficulties with the latter are now clear. Before deeming them necessary evils in the struggle to overcome pervasive prejudice, why not try scrupulous enforcement of procedural affirmative action? We might thereby most directly achieve that equitable society so ardently desired by every person of good will.

IO

Complexities of Affirmative Action

AFFIRMATIVE ACTION HAS REMAINED a divisive issue in the United States for a half-century.[1] Indeed, during that time opinion polls have remained remarkably stable, indicating that approximately half the public supports affirmative action while the other half opposes it.

Yet procedural affirmative action is not controversial. Few oppose announcing positions openly, banning any racial, religious, ethnic, or gender tests for candidates, and eliminating from all procedures any policies that harbor prejudice, however vestigial.

The source of the debate, however, is preferential affirmative action, which calls for making special efforts to recruit individuals who meet institutional goals related to racial, gender, or ethnic identity. Announce any program of this sort, and the heat of the debate will soon become intense.

Part of the problem is that advocates of preferential affirmative action, which I shall henceforth refer to simply as affirmative action, do not share one rationale. Is the aim to offset past discrimination, counteract present unfairness, or achieve future equality?

---

1. The full range of historical and contemporary arguments can be found in *The Affirmative Action Debate*, Second Edition, ed. Steven M. Cahn (New York and London: Routledge, 2002).

The first is often referred to as "compensation," the second as "a level playing field," and the third as "diversity."

Note that each of these can be defended independently of the others. Compensation for past wrongs may be owed, although at present the playing field is level and diversity is not sought. Ot the playing field at present may not be level, although compensation for past wrongs is not owed and future diversity is not sought. Or future diversity may be sought, although compensation for past wrongs is not owed and presently the planning field is level.

Perhaps all three factors might be relevant, but each requires a different justification and calls for a different remedy. In particular, past wrongs would be offset if suitable compensation was made, but once provided to the appropriate recipients, no other steps would be needed. Present wrongs would be corrected if actions were taken that would level the playing field, but doing so would be consistent with unequal outcomes. Future equality would require continuing attention to ensure that an appropriate balance, once achieved, would never be lost. Thus, defenders of affirmative action would likely favor at least one of these policies but not necessarily more than one.

Nowadays the most frequently cited defense of affirmative action is an appeal to diversity. That term, however, requires a modifier, such as racial diversity, gender diversity, religious diversity, and so on. Without this clarification, unmodified diversity fails to be a useful concept.

To highlight the problem, imagine a ten-person philosophy department that has no Black, no woman, no person under fifty, no non-Christian, no registered Republican, none whose doctoral degree is from other than an Ivy League university, none who served in a war, none who is gay, none who was ever on welfare, none who is physically challenged, none whose work is outside the analytic tradition, and none who specializes in aesthetics. When the next appointment is made, which characteristics should be stressed so as to render this department more diverse? I know of no compelling answer.

To put the matter more vividly, suppose that the ten finalists for a position in that department include a Black, a woman, a thirty-year-old, a Buddhist, a Republican, someone whose doctoral degree is from Indiana University, a veteran, someone who was once on welfare, someone who uses a wheelchair, a lesbian, a specialist in continental philosophy, and an aesthetician. Which should be favored purely on grounds of enhancing diversity? The question is unanswerable.

Another complicating feature of affirmative action is its call for giving preference to members of certain groups. But what sort of preference is urged?

For example, imagine a search for an assistant professor in which one hundred persons apply, and among them are some who are members of a group designated for affirmative action. Let us refer to them as AA candidates. Suppose the dean has permitted five applicants to be invited for campus interviews. After studying all the vitae and sets of recommendations, the department ranks ten candidates as outstanding, twenty as good, fifty as merely qualified, and twenty as unqualified. Let us suppose that four applicants are AA candidates, and among them one is ranked as outstanding, one as good, one as merely qualified, and one as unqualified.

The key question is: Assuming AA candidates are to be preferred, what forms of preference are called for? One possibility is to interview any AA candidate who is outstanding, regardless of the merits of any other outstanding candidates. Another possibility is to interview any AA candidate who is good, even though some candidates are stronger. Yet another possibility is to agree to interview any AA candidate who is qualified, even though most candidates are stronger. A theoretical possibility is to interview even unqualified AA candidates, although I know of no one who would support that policy, so let us set it aside. What remains are three different models of preference, any of which might be defended.

Next assume two AA candidates are chosen for interviews, one who was ranked as outstanding and another as good. Afterwards, the department places the outstanding candidate second and the other fifth. Does giving preference to AA candidates require that the second candidate be offered the position? And if the candidate ranked second receives a more attractive offer and withdraws from consideration, need the candidate now ranked fifth be preferred?

Of course, an AA candidate may be ranked the highest, thus avoiding any problems. Otherwise, the call for giving preference requires an interpretation that is rarely, if ever, announced ahead of time.

Thus far my discussion has centered on faculty appointments, but different considerations may arise in justifying affirmative action in student admissions. After all, colleges traditionally take account of a high school applicant's athletic prowess, community service, personal relationships to alumni, and geographic home. Such criteria, however, are not considered in a faculty search. No wonder defenders of affirmative action are most comfortable supporting it in the context of a complex admissions decision involving many non-academic factors, while opponents most often think of the policy in relation to assessing the research and teaching of applicants for faculty positions. The two decisions are different in kind, and the same arguments may not apply to both.

In addition, circumstances matter. Consider a department that has never appointed a woman and, when given a promising opportunity, refuses even to interview one. Suppose the dean insists that in the next search process some women should be interviewed, and if a woman with a superlative record is found, she should be appointed. Would opponents of affirmative action object? I think not.

On the other hand, consider a department that announces its intention to achieve a goal of fifty percent women, and in its next search prefers a minimally qualified women to a man who is far more promising as a researcher, teacher, and contributor to the life of the department. If the dean insists that the man be appointed, would proponents of affirmative action be upset? Again, I think not.

Both these cases are admittedly extreme, although not entirely unrealistic, but the lesson is that presuming affirmative action to be at odds with merit, as its opponents do, or to be a means of obtaining justice, as its defenders do, are oversimplifications. The context matters.

In conclusion, I recognize that I have not supported or opposed affirmative action. As it turns out, however, that decision depends on whether the goal is compensation, a level playing field, or diversity; what sorts of diversity are sought; what sorts of preference are proposed; whether the focus is faculty appointments or student admissions; and whether any special circumstances are part of the context. Without that information, taking an unconditional position for or against affirmative action suggests a failure to appreciate the matter's complexities.

II

A Puzzle

SUPPOSE YOUR DEPARTMENT HAS no faculty members from a particular racial or ethnic group. In the past, some members of the group have applied but none has been chosen. A representative of your school's Board of Trustees consults you about a proposal, currently under consideration by the Board, to fund a professorship in your department open only to scholars from that racial or ethnic group. Would you support this idea?

If you do, would you agree that the announcement of the position should inform potential applicants of its special feature so that all can decide whether to apply in light of full information about the search? After all, the plan is presumably within moral and legal bounds. Why, then, not state the policy without equivocation?

Facing the usual practice of keeping such information under wraps, Tom L. Beauchamp wrote:

> Incompleteness in advertising sometimes stems from fear of legal liability but more often from fear of departmental embarrassment and harm either to reputation or to future recruiting efforts.
>
> The greater moral embarrassment, however, is that we academics fear making public what we believe to be morally commendable and mandatory in our recruiting efforts. There is something deeply wrong in this

circumstance, one that virtually every academic department now faces.[1]

But what, if anything, is "deeply wrong"? Is it the proposed practice, the law, the lack of moral courage on the part of faculty or administrators, or something else?

1. Tom L. Beauchamp, "Quotas by Any Name: Some Problems of Affirmative Action in Faculty Appointments," in Cahn, 215.

PART IV

A Teacher's Responsibilities

12

Caring about Students

YEARS AGO AT A meeting of the American Philosophical Association, I passed a group of graduate students who were responding enthusiastically as one described a position for which he had just been interviewed. "It's a great job," he told his friends. "There's very little teaching, and I'll have plenty of time for my work." I wish someone had informed him that, in fact, teaching *was* his work.

He might have responded, however, that many highly regarded professors only grudgingly give time or attention to the classroom. Instead, they concentrate on their own scholarship.

In that regard, consider a professor I once knew who enjoyed a strong reputation for his research. Yet he regularly cancelled classes. He arrived late when he did attend and was often unprepared. He constructed no examinations so that he would have none to correct. In each course, he assigned one term paper. If he liked the first few pages, he gave the student an A for the course; if he wasn't impressed, he gave a B. Those who didn't submit a paper received a C. This grading system avoided most complaints, although occasionally a student who had been given a B would grumble. The matter would be settled quickly, though, by the instructor's graciously changing the B to an A.

Surely this celebrated scholar was unethical. He was akin to a corrupt corporate executive or a crooked judge. He held an honorable title but abused the responsibilities of his position.

Fortunately, more professors than might be supposed act wholly otherwise. They are deeply concerned whether their students become interested in the subject, grasp assigned readings, understand explanations offered in class, and view as reasonable policies regarding assignments, examinations, and grades.

Why do these instructor's care? They recognize that teaching has a moral dimension because students can be helped or harmed by their educational experience. Thus, conscientious faculty take seriously pedagogic duties.

Now let's return to a variation on the story with which I began. Suppose you go to a doctor's office and overhear the physicians discussing with zest the possibility that one of them might be fortunate enough to obtain a laboratory position that would not involve seeing any patients. As you listen, you realize that these practitioners are concerned primarily with their own research, not with your personal medical problems. In such circumstances, most of us would seek doctors who are more eager to provide help. Likewise, students respond negatively to any professor who by word or deed reflects the attitude that teaching is merely a distraction from the essence of the academic enterprise.

Nevertheless, a colleague might ask skeptically, "Why should I put effort into classes when doing so doesn't advance my career?" Here is a version of the familiar challenge "Why should I be moral?" Whatever the reply, if a professor doesn't care about students, then they are the losers.

13

Every Student Counts

YEARS AGO, THE DEPARTMENT of which I was then a member invited to campus a promising candidate for a faculty position. He had been highly recommended based in part on his purported pedagogical skills, but after listening to him present a convoluted talk, I had doubts. Later, as he recounted his success in teaching introductory philosophy, I asked him to estimate the percentage of students in the class who understood his lectures. "Definitely half," he replied proudly. When I inquired about the other half, he answered that they were not philosophically sophisticated enough to follow the arguments. No wonder, given my department's commitment to excellence in teaching, he was not offered a position.

We all recognize that some students are stronger than others, and often the temptation is to focus on the standouts. The aim of teaching, however, is not to please instructors but to enlighten students, And although some may be difficult to reach, all who are trying to learn should be offered help in doing so. Remember, every student who has registered for the course deserves attention, and teachers are obligated to provide it. After all, most students have the ability to succeed, assuming their instructor is capable and cares about their progress.

Concern for all students is compatible with reaching out to the strongest, perhaps by offering them in-class challenges or extra-credit assignments. In truth, though, the talented do not need more help than others. Do you suppose Plato was worried whether he could keep Aristotle's attention?

While few professors underestimate how much their students are learning, many instructors overestimate. They are dismayed when examination papers display egregious misunderstanding and are apt to disparage students whose work contains simple errors. A likely explanation for the phenomenon, however, is that the instruction was inadequate. Professors dissatisfied with the performance of their students may take refuge in supposing that the material lies beyond their grasp, but as Tamar Szabó Gendler, Dean of the Faculty of Arts and Sciences at Yale University, once remarked to me, any subject can be explained successfully if you know how.

The challenge of effective teaching is to reach not only those students who come to class with enthusiasm and continually raise their hands to participate. Rather, the key is whether you can appeal to students who arrive in class with little interest and seemingly limited talent. The crucial question is this: Can you excite these students about the material and enhance their knowledge and skills?

Admittedly, doing so is difficult. Yet good teachers sometimes succeed, and great teachers often do. Granted, even the finest instructors fail occasionally, but in that case, they are likely to express dissatisfaction not with their students but with themselves.

When candidates at interviews are asked about the extent of their success in the classroom, I have little confidence in anyone who replies, "I don't think too much about teaching, but mine's okay." Instead, I hope to hear, "I believe I reach most of the students, but I'm always trying to reach all of them." The most unsatisfying answer, which I have heard too often, is "I work well with good students." In that case, I am tempted to respond, "Who doesn't?"

14

Grading

MANY TEACHERS ARE UNCOMFORTABLE with grades, viewing them as inherently inaccurate devices that, in attempting to measure people, only traumatize and dehumanize them. This concern, however, is a tangle of misconceptions.

A grade represents an expert's judgment of the quality of a student's work in a specific course. As such, it can serve not only to determine whether students are making satisfactory progress or earning academic honors but also to aid students themselves in judging their past efforts and formulating their future plans.

Would these functions be better served if, as some have suggested, grades were replaced by letters of evaluation? In addition to the impracticality of a professor's writing hundreds of individual comments and evaluators reading thousands, the value of such letters would be severely limited if they didn't include specific indications of students' level of performance—in other words, grades. Otherwise, the letters would be more likely to reveal the teachers' literary styles than the students' academic accomplishments. Remarks one instructor considers high praise may be used indiscriminately by another, while comments intended as mild commendation might be mistaken for tempered criticism.

While a piece of work would not necessarily be graded identically by all specialists, those in the same department usually agree whether a student's performance has been outstanding, good, fair, poor, or unsatisfactory, the levels of achievement typically symbolized by A, B, C, D, F. Granted, experts sometimes disagree, but in doing so they do not obliterate the distinction between their knowledgeable judgments and a novice's uninformed impressions.

What of the oft-repeated charge that grades are impersonal devices that reduce people to letters of the alphabet? That criticism is misguided. A grade is not a measure of a person but of a person's level of achievement in a particular course. A student who receives a grade of C in introductory French is not a C person with a C personality or C moral character but one whose performance in introductory French was acceptable but not distinguished. Perhaps the student will do much better in later courses and may eventually excel in the study of French literature, but this first try was not highly successful.

Whether grades are fair, however, depends on a teacher's conscientiousness in assigning them. One potential misuse is to award grades on bases other than a student's level of achievement. Irrelevant criteria include a student's gender, race, nationality, physical appearance, dress, personality, attitudes, innate capacities, and previous academic record. None of these factors should even be considered in deciding a student's grade. Performance in the course should be the only criterion.

If an A in symbolic logic might mean that the student tried hard, came from an impoverished community, or displayed an ingratiating personality, then the A is hopelessly ambiguous and serves no purpose. If, on the other hand, the grade signifies that the student has a firm grasp of the essentials of symbolic logic, then the message is clear.

The most effective means for ensuring that no extraneous factors enter grading is for the instructor to clarify at the beginning of the term how final grades will be determined. How much will the final examination count? How about the papers and other short assignments? Will the student's participation be a factor? Answering these questions at the outset enables students to concentrate their energies on the most important aspects of the course, not waste time speculating about the instructor's intentions.

Yet if the announced system is unnecessarily complicated, it can distort the purpose of the course. For example, if the instructor announces that to receive an A you need to accumulate 965 points out of 1000, and the final exam is worth 350, each of the other two exams is worth 120, each of the two papers is worth 140, and class discussion is worth 130, the class has taken on the appearance of a complicated game show. The rule of thumb should be this: Explain your grading system but keep matters simple.

The most common misuse of grades is the practice commonly referred to as "grading on a curve." The essence of this scheme is for the instructor to decide before the course begins what percentage of students will receive each grade. This method will produce aesthetically pleasing designs on a graph but is nevertheless conceptually confused. While a student's achievement should be judged in the light of reasonable expectations, these do not depend on such haphazard circumstances as the mix of students taking the course concurrently.

Consider the plight of a student who earns an 80 on an exam but receives a D because most classmates scored higher. Yet the following semester in the same course, another earns an 80 with the same answers and receives an A because this time almost all classmates scored lower. Two students, identical work, different grades: the system is patently unfair.

Years ago I overheard a student complain to his instructor about receiving a B. This nationally known scholar responded sympathetically but explained with regret that all the A grades were taken. His scholarly skills far exceeded his pedagogical wisdom.

Why do so many instructors resort to this approach? By so doing they avoid responsibility for determining the level of work each grade represents. They are also free to construct examinations without concern for skewed results because even if the highest grade is 30 out of 100, grading on a curve will yield apparently acceptable consequences. Yet the appearance is deceiving because class rank will have been conflated with subject mastery. The

Procrustean practice of grading on a curve rests on this muddle and should be abandoned, although inept teaching or badly constructed examinations should not result in unconscionably low grades.

A different distortion of the grading system, rare today, is an unwillingness to award high grades. Instructors who adopt this attitude take pride in rigor. But just as a third-grade student who receives an A in mathematics need not be the equal of Isaac Newton, so a first-year college student may receive an A in writing without being the equal of George Orwell. Receiving an A only means that, judged by reasonable standards, the student has done excellent work. An instructor who rarely rewards high grades is failing to distinguish good from poor performance. Doing so does not uphold academic standards but only misinterprets the grading symbols, thereby undermining their appropriate functions.

A more common misuse of the system is the reluctance to award low grades, a practice popularly known as "grade inflation." It results from the unwillingness of instructors to give students the bad news that they have not done as well as they might have hoped. Yet maintaining academic standards rests on the willingness of professors to tell the truth.

Understandably, some are concerned about the possible injustice of giving their own students realistic grades while other students receive inflated ones. The solution adopted at some colleges is for transcripts to include not only a student's course grade but also the average grade for all those in the course. In this way grade inflation is exposed and unfairness dissipated. In any case, each instructor who inflates grades adds to the problem.

Awarding grades also calls for a sense of fair play. Consider a teacher I knew who gave relatively easy exams throughout the semester, thereby leading students to believe they were doing well. The final examination, however, was vastly more difficult, and many students were shocked and angered to receive low grades for the course. Clearly, this instructor misled and harmed his students; he was akin to a storeowner who announces a major sale but fools customers by applying low prices to only a few rarely sought items.

Grading is especially sensitive to mishandling because assessments are done privately and results are not easily challenged. Teachers, therefore, need to make every effort to treat students equitably. Morality requires no less.

15

A Teacher's Role

TEACHERS ARE RESPONSIBLE FOR guiding the learning process. They should be expected to know which material is to be studied and in what order it is best presented. They should also understand how a student can proceed most productively, what constitutes individual progress, and when someone has achieved it.

Suppose you enroll in an introductory course in chess and your instructor begins by inquiring whether the class would prefer to learn first how rooks move or when castling is permitted. Such a question would be senseless, for a reasonable answer depends on some knowledge of chess, and if you already had that, you wouldn't be in a class for beginners.

With responsibility goes authority. We speak not only of authority as power but also of *an* authority, that is, an expert. The two concepts are related, for the responsibilities that entail the exercise of authority or power are typically assigned to individuals by virtue of their presumed authority or expertise.

Such is the case with teachers, for their superior knowledge justifies their being assigned pedagogic responsibilities. After all, if teachers understand a subject no better than their students, why should students be charged tuition while teachers receive paychecks? I have often heard teachers minimize their own importance and emphasize how much they learned from their students, but I have yet to hear a single professor offer to exchange an instructor's salary for a student's bill.

To recognize a teacher's authority, however, is not to suggest that the teacher should act in an authoritarian manner. The appropriate relationship is that of guide, not god. Guides are expected to be familiar with the areas through which they lead you, pointing out highlights and warning of dangers. They are to blame if you follow their instructions but miss important sites or fall victim to a peril that should have been anticipated. The guide who responds to charges of incompetence by blaming the visitors' lack of knowledge is not thereby relieved of responsibility.

Recognizing the extent to which students are necessarily dependent on their instructors leads to the realization of how much damage faculty members can inflict. Which of us has not felt the sting of a teacher's thoughtless gibe? Or been victimized by carelessness or meanness? Or developed an aversion to some subject as a result of a teacher's incompetent, tedious, or aberrant presentation? In short, the teacher has the capacity to help or harm students. Achieving the former and avoiding the latter are the primary responsibilities of every instructor.

A teacher may be especially challenged by a student who is emotionally unstable. In that case, teachers, however well-intentioned, should not try to practice clinical psychology. Rather, those students dealing with a personal difficulty should be advised to visit the school's counseling service where professionals are qualified to deal with such matters.

Yet the most egregious instances of professorial malfeasance rest on the mistaken supposition that teachers ought to be friends with their students. What is wrong with this approach, as Sidney Hook pointed out, is that "teachers must be friendly without becoming a friend, although [they] may pave the way for later friendship, for friendship is a mark of preference and expresses itself in indulgence, favors, and distinctions that unconsciously find an invidious form."[1] Faculty ought to care about the progress of each

---

1. Sidney Hook, *Education for Modern Man: A New Perspective* (1963; Eugene, OR: Wipf and Stock Publishers, 2020), 230–231.

student, but they should remain dispassionate, able to deliberate, judge, and act without thought of personal interest or advantage. Even the appearance of partiality is likely to impair the learning process by damaging an instructor's credibility, causing students to doubt that standards are being applied fairly.

Every teacher should scrupulously avoid giving any students preferential treatment. If one student is permitted to write a paper instead of taking an examination, that option should be available to everyone in the class. If one is allowed to turn in assignment late, then all others in like circumstances should be offered the same opportunity. And if one is invited to the professor's home for dinner, then everyone should receive similar invitations. Adherence to this guideline never leads to trouble; breaking it is often problematic.

One obvious implication of the principle of equal consideration is that between teacher and student not only is friendship inappropriate but even more so is romance. Even if a student never enrolls in a professor's classes, their liaison suggests that this faculty member does not view students from a professional standpoint. If an attempt is made to keep the relationship secret, the professor's integrity is compromised. In any case, such efforts at concealment almost always fail, thereby besmirching the professor's reputation for honesty.

Should a student seek to initiate an affair with a professor, the only proper response is an unequivocal refusal. On the other hand, for a professor to attempt to seduce or coerce a student is an egregious abuse of authority that provides strong grounds for dismissal.

When a student has left the college or moved to a different unit of the university, whatever personal contact may develop with a professor is up to the two of them. During the years of undergraduate or graduate study, however, the only appropriate relationship is professional. To maintain these bounds is in everyone's best interest, and no less so in the context of scholarly collaboration.

For whatever reasons, academics have recently had more than their share of scandals involving forms of sexual harassment or abuse. Under these unfortunate circumstances, teachers should be especially vigilant to maintain their proper function as guides through a field of study. They should not seek or accept the role of psychiatrist, friend, or lover. Overstepping these bounds likely leads to a moral quagmire.

16

The Call of Duty

ABOUT THREE DECADES AGO, I served on the jury in a highly publicized, double-murder case. The defendant was a mother who was charged with killing her two newborns and attempting to kill her third. In court she admitted the crimes but pleaded insanity. The trial took several weeks, with dueling psychologists offering conflicting testimony. At the end, the jury was sequestered during its two days of deliberation, and eventually the defendant was found not guilty by reason of mental disease or defect.

While I still recall many of the details, what I remember most vividly is the seriousness of the jury in carrying out its responsibilities. From the moment we entered the courtroom and saw the accused sitting with her lawyer at the defendant's table, the weight of the situation affected us deeply. The other jurors and I listened carefully to the judge's instructions and made every effort to carry out our duties as scrupulously as possible. A woman's life hung in the balance, and our responsibility was to ensure that justice was done. After the verdict was announced, we were pleased when several officers of the court came to the jury room to thank us for our service and indicate that they believed we had reached the most appropriate decision.

Most importantly, although we were forced to endure a variety of inconveniences, we realized that the proceedings had not been planned to suit us. We were being asked to make a momentous judgment and were expected to do so as conscientiously as possible, regardless of our personal preferences about the process.

Let me now contrast this experience with an occasion many years before when my brother and I took a cruise to Nassau. From the moment our ship left the dock until the time we returned, the crew made every effort to cater to our wishes. Food and drink were available at our request, and innumerable activities were arranged for our pleasure. We were the focus of attention, and the aim of the enterprise was to fulfill as many of our wishes as possible. Of course, the hope was that we would find the experience a positive one and register for additional cruises. Although I never did because I found the rocking of the ship to be unsettling, I admit that having your expressed desires fulfilled without delay by an amiable crew is delightful.

Now I ask: As a college teacher, do you expect the experience to be more like serving on a jury or taking a cruise? In other words, do you expect administrators and colleagues to seek every opportunity to satisfy your desires, or do you anticipate that the obligation to guide students and treat them equitably will weigh on your conscience and temper your enjoyment?

For example, suppose you are asked to share office space when you would prefer to have your own. Or you are given a Monday, Wednesday, Friday course schedule, although you would rather not teach on Fridays. Or you are asked to offer a course that is not your first or second choice. Or faculty meetings occur at inopportune times.

If you are expecting to be a passenger on an academic cruise, then you will be greatly upset by these inconveniences. But if you think of yourself as a member of an academic jury, then these matters will assume fair less importance. After all, as a juror, the room in which you meet may be cramped and windowless. The court's schedule may be inconvenient, and you may spend hours waiting for the trial to proceed. You will be required to forego reading any newspapers or watching any media that might contain relevant stories. You may even be sequestered for a time, cut off from home and family. Yet a person's life or welfare may hang in the balance, and hence you put aside every annoyance and concentrate instead on fulfilling the duties you swore to uphold.

As a faculty member, you also assume serious responsibilities, and while you may rarely think of the matter in these terms, your actions may put students at risk. Granted, professors are not usually in position to affect the life of any individual to the extent a jury might, but the activities of professors ultimately affect the life of an entire society, strengthening or weakening its members' skills in reasoning, interpretation, and evaluation.

Thus, joining a faculty is far closer to serving on a jury than taking a cruise, for professors owe the community every effort to replace ignorance and prejudice with understanding and fair-mindedness. Such is the obligation of faculty members, and they should be prepared to take pains and shoulder burdens trying to fulfill it.

17

Gratitude

ONE NOTICEABLE FEATURE OF academic life is how much time is spent arguing against the views of others. After all, for a paper to be thought worthy of presentation or an article to be considered publishable, it needs to express at least some dissatisfaction with prevailing opinion.

Such a focus upon finding fault readily diminishes empathy. For example, years ago I attended a departmental colloquium where the speaker offered a talk that I found clear, insightful, and compelling. When the time came for comments, I expressed appreciation for her fine presentation. The audience waited for my criticisms, but I had none. I merely wanted to offer a compliment. My attitude, however, appeared to shock my colleagues. Wasn't I going to try to demonstrate the limitations of her approach? Wasn't I going to call attention to a reference she had omitted? If not, why had I spoken?

Similarly, I recall that soon after the publication of the late Robert Nozick's remarkable book *Philosophical Explanations* I saw him at a national meeting of the American Philosophical Association where I told him how much I admired his new work.[1] Then, however, I apologized for repeating what he had surely heard

1. Robert Nozick, *Philosophical Explanations* (Cambridge, MA: Harvard University Press, 1981).

many times before. To my surprise he replied ruefully that, in fact, I was the first person there to have complimented him. Other had sought him out, but only to express disagreement; no word of encouragement had passed their lips.

Not offering appreciation when merited indicates a lack of manners, a failure to treat others appropriately. The link between manners and ethics was noted by Thomas Hobbes, who referred to manners as small morals,[2] an insight John Dewey expressed more alliteratively by stating that "manners are but minor morals."[3]

Academics may be prone to overlook the connection because too many view scholarly inquiry as a competition in which you score points by refuting others rather than a cooperative enterprise in which participants reason together to enhance understanding. Indeed, whenever colleagues move the process forward, they deserve thanks.

Appreciation should also extend to students. However unsophisticated their remarks may be, so long as they are trying to contribute to the discussion, they deserve encouragement.

Neither rudeness nor arrogance belongs in a classroom. Instead of an instructor's reacting to a student's opinion by declaring, "You've missed an obvious point," a more appropriate reply would be something like this, "You may be on to something, but let's consider a possible objection to your view."

Just as a response to a student's question should display appreciation for the effort to participate, similarly when comments are offered at a professional lecture, they should begin on a positive note, even if only to thank the speaker for raising provocative issues. Such politeness will not diminish the significance of any challenge offered but will reinforce the principle that criticism is consistent with courtesy.

2. Thomas Hobbes, *Leviathan* (Cleveland and New York: The World Publishing Company,1963), 122.

3. John Dewey, *Democracy and Education: The Middle Works of John Dewey*, 1899–1924, ed. Jo Ann Boydston (Carbondale, IL.: Southern Illinois University Press, 1980), 9:22.

Academic life has its share of travails. These would be lessened, however, if professors emphasized not only the importance of correctness but also a concern for kindness.

About the Author

STEVEN M. CAHN IS Professor Emeritus of Philosophy at the City University of New York Graduate Center, where he served for nearly a decade as Provost and Vice President for Academic Affairs, then as Acting President.

He was born in Springfield, Massachusetts, in 1942. His younger years were devoted to music, and he studied piano with Herbert Stessin of the Juilliard School and the noted chamber music artist Artur Balsam. He also became a professional organist under the tutelage of the well-known composer Isadore Freed.

After earning an AB from Columbia College in 1963 and PhD in philosophy from Columbia University in 1966, Dr. Cahn taught at Dartmouth College, Vassar College, New York University, the University of Rochester, and the University of Vermont, where he chaired the Department of Philosophy and led the successful effort to build what remains one of the nation's most highly rated undergraduate philosophy programs.

He served as a program officer at the Exxon Education Foundation, as Acting Director for Humanities at the Rockefeller Foundation, and as the first Director of General Programs at the National Endowment for the Humanities. He formerly chaired the American Philosophical Association's Committee on the Teaching of Philosophy, was the Association's delegate to the American Council of Learned Societies, and was longtime President of the John Dewey Foundation, where he proposed and brought to fruition the John Dewey Lectures, now delivered at every national meeting of the American Philosophical Association.

He has presented numerous addresses at colleges and universities throughout the United States, including the first Naumberg Memorial Lecture at UCLA, the Minerva Lecture at Union College, the convocation address at Florida International University, and a keynote speech to the Kenan Convocation at the University of North Carolina at Chapel Hill. He has also spoken on the subject of academic ethics to many organizations, among them the College Entrance Examination Board, the American Board of Internal Medicine, the New England Association of Schools and Colleges, the American Association of State Colleges and Universities, the National Association of Academic Affairs Administrators, and both the Northeastern and Midwestern Associations of Graduate Schools.

Dr. Cahn is the author of over twenty books, including *Fate, Logic, and Time, Religion Within Reason, Philosophical Adventures, A Philosopher's Journey: Essays from Six Decades,* and *Philosophical Debates.* He has also edited more than fifty books, including *Exploring Philosophy of Religion* (now in its second edition), *Political Philosophy* (now in its fourth edition), *Exploring Ethics* (now in its sixth edition), *Exploring Philosophy* (now in its eighth edition), and *Classics of Western Philosophy* (now in its eighth edition). He has also served as general editor of four multivolume series: *Blackwell Philosophy Guides; Blackwell Readings in Philosophy; Issues in Academic Ethics,* and *Critical Essays on the Classics.*

His numerous articles have appeared in a broad spectrum of publications, including *The Journal of Philosophy, The Chronicle of Higher Education, Shakespeare Newsletter, The American Journal of Medicine, The New Republic,* and *The New York Times.*

A collection of essays written in his honor, edited by two of his former doctoral students, Robert B. Talisse of Vanderbilt University and Maureen Eckert of the University of Massachusetts Dartmouth, is titled *A Teacher's Life: Essays for Steven M. Cahn.* His professional autobiography appears in his book *The Road Traveled and Other Essays.*

Index

academic ethics, field of, xii–xv
Academic Ethics Today, xiv, xv
academic freedom and tenure, 32
academic politics and academic
    requirements, 11–13
academic quality and tenure, 40
academic requirements, 11–13.
    See also distribution
    requirements
Acampora, Christa Davis, xiv
advisory system, 4–5
aesthetic experience, sensitivity
    to, 9
affirmative action
    compensatory advantage,
        55–56, 60, 66, 69
    complexities, 65–69
    concepts of, 53–64
    faculty search process, 61–63
    group role models, 62–63
    incompleteness in hiring
        advertisements, 70–71
    irrelevant criteria, 60–61
    level playing field, 66, 69
    meaning of term, 53
    preferential, 55–56, 60, 65,
        67–68
    procedural, 54, 64, 65
    stereotyping, 56, 62
    student admissions process,
        68–69
Aikin, Scott F., xiv

Allen, Anita L., xiv
American Association of University
    Professors, 38
appointments. *See* faculty
    appointments
appreciation. *See* gratitude
    (teacher's)
arts, study of, 24–26
Audi, Robert, xii
Austin, J.L., 16

bachelor's degree and science
    requirements, 11–12
Bakke decision, 56n3
Banditt, Theodore M., xii
Beauchamp, Tom L., 70
Becker, Lawrence C., xii
"blind review," 34–35
Bok, Derek, xiv
Bowen, William G., xiv
Bradner, Alexandra, xiv
Brand, Myles, xiv
Brann, Eva T.H., 6
Brighouse, Harry, xv
Brown University, 3

City University of New York, 12, 59
Civil Rights Act, 54
class size, 13, 45, 47
colleagues
    constructive criticism, 91–92
    gratitude to, 92

97

Tuana, Nancy, xiv
Tyranny of Testing, The (Hoffman), 57–58

underutilization, concept of, 55
University of Vermont, 11–12
U.S. Department of Labor, 54–55

voting. *See* departmental voting

Warnick, Bryan, xiv–xv
Western civilization, study of, 12, 20–22
Wilcox, Shelley, xiv
Williams College, 14
Wolf-Devine, Cecia, 62
Wolff, Robert Paul, xiv
world history, study of, 9

Yale College, 53n1

www.ingramcontent.com/pod-product-compliance
Lightning Source LLC
Chambersburg PA
CBHW071051090426
42737CB00013B/2322